After Schooling

A Guide

Ekeh Joe Obinna

Machine Creative
75 Venn South Onitsha Anambra State, Nigeria.

Copyright © Ekeh Joe Obinna 2015
All rights reserved. Without limiting the rights under copyright reserved above, no part of this publication may be reproduced, stored or introduced into a retrieval system, or transmitted, in any form or by any means (electronic, mechanical, photocopying, recording or otherwise), without the prior written permission of the copyright owner only.

ISBN: 978-978-945-628-4
Published in Nigeria in 2015
Under the Management of Ceno Ventures Ltd
#75 Venn Road South Onitsha, Anambra State, Nigeria.

Disclaimer: Reasonable care has been taken to ensure that the information presented in this book is accurate. However, the reader should understand that the information provided does not constitute any legal, medical, or professional advice of any kind.

Companies, organizations, products, pictures, stories, and individuals mentioned in this book are used for identification and illustrative purposes only. The user or reader, however, accepts that the author does not attempt to criticise, report, accuse, support, gossip, estimate, or present the subject matter for further investigation. However, the author who is the producer of 'The Twenty-Two Laws of Enduring Success' understands that it may not work for everybody. Therefore, If you should find this book in your possession, you are advised to consider it as none general strategy.

This book is supplied "as is" without warranties. All warranties, expressed or implied, are here disclaimed. Therefore, use of this book constitutes acceptance of the "No Liability" policy.

If you do not agree with this policy, you are not permitted to use or distribute this book. Ekeh Joe Obinna, distributors, and agents shall not be liable for any losses or damage whatsoever (including, without limitation, consequential loss or damage) directly or indirectly arising from the use of this book.

Author	**Ekeh Joe Obinna**
	(Author of other books)
Country	Nigeria
Language	English
	Other Languages (***** ** *** **** ******)
Subject	Self Development, Personal Success, Self Help, Entrepreneurship, Business, Investing, Economics.
Director	**Onuoha Anthony**
	(Counselling) UNN.
	(Economics) FCE, COE, Abuja.
Published	January 2015
ISBN	10 (978-945-628-X)
	13 (978-978-945-628-4)
Foreword	**Agoha Bob Ifeanyi**
	(Head, International Liaison & Outreach, The Electoral Institute, INEC, Nigeria)
Asst. Researcher	**Ekeh Blessing Ifunanya**
	(Information Scientist)
Editor	Chinwendu Chukwuneke
Management	**Ekeh Joe Obinna Machine Creative. Ceno Ventures Ltd**
	#75 Venn Road South Onitsha, Anambra State, Nigeria.
	+234 (0) 8063077041

Please address questions and book requests to:
Ceno Ventures Ltd.
No.75 Venn Road South Onitsha, Anambra State, Nigeria.
Phone: **+2348063077041(Author)**
Email: machine_u@yahoo.com

DEDICATION

To God who gives the **PERFECT** dream,
To my Family (Parents) who show me the **PERFECT** way,
To my Friends who have the **PERFECT** job,
To my Government who gives us the **PERFECT** right and freedom,
And to Youths who give the **PERFECT** service for a **PERFECT** pay.

ACKNOWLEDGMENT

I am indeed grateful to my country, Nigeria, for providing the citizens (both citizens by birth, citizens by registration, citizens by naturalization or otherwise) with equal rights and freedom to accumulate wealth and riches to any possible height with no/little tax; to LearnVest Planning Service, United State of America; to www.pbs.org; to members of Co-Creators Universe (NGO); to all the members of Igbo Council of Commerce, Access Bank Plc and all its business alliance, Ceno Ventures Ltd, Fidelity Bank Plc and all its business alliance, Franko Bookshop: Sir Jezz, and to Institute of Management and Technology (IMT) Enugu.

I am not forgetting Nigeria corps members who dedicate their resources to call of civilization, to one or two worthy ends. I acknowledge you, Director-General, Brig. Gen. Johnson Olawumi of National Youth Service Corps, I appeal that you will enhance the entrepreneurial development and other poverty alleviation initiatives implemented by Brig. Gen. Nnamdi Okore-Affia, former National Youth Service Corps' Director-General. All the members of staff of National Youth Service Corps, I commend you.

Mrs. Chinwendu Chukwuneke I must not fail to commend you. Mr. Agoha I. C, Sapele Zonal Inspector, National Youth Service Corps, Delta State, thank you; Mrs. Chinwe F. Ojukwu, 2012-State Coordinator, National Youth Service Corps, Imo State, thank you for the orientation; Postulant Friday Richard Ossi, former Church Teacher, Church of the Resurrection, Anglican Church, Woliwo Layout Onitsha, Anambra State of Nigeria, thank you.

Thank you Ekeh Joe Obinna.

FOREWORD

It has been my privilege for some years to address regularly, in a very different understanding, the issue of unemployment in different themes and foray. I have lectured to a class of students on the subject matter; and in number of times, I have lectured to an audience consisting of employees, business men and women on subjects of 'Moral' and 'Achievement'. I cannot say that this collocation ever appeared as a different thing to myself, but certainly for our Nation, Parents, Leaders, Friends, they see the fate as more than a problem.

I looked around this fate of unemployment and saw a monster. Years ago, I looked for the answer and I saw dark shadows. They lay at different poles of thought. This answer could not be seen, it could not be touched, it could not be smelled, but it was just there. I saw it within the rich and the poor, the employed and the unemployed. I saw a reasonable answer, but out of duties toward the natural authorities, a large number of youths are in the hands of a piercing flame of insufficient job opportunity and they are suffering and being delayed from manifesting their innate potentials. There are commandments, unknown to many, which have made lots of youths step backward. It is only nature that has a lasting answer to the fate of unemployment.

Today, I have seen a book which expresses, in sincerity of truth, the same observation which I also made years ago. This little volume of book is indeed written, as a result of long time of reasonable research, meditation, and years of learning. It is simply suggestive, and to large extent prescriptive. Properly observe the simple rules. There is no successful man or woman that has not pass through it. It will also be good if you understand that you should not adopt some and despise the other. It's aimed to stimulate men and women of different professions to the understanding and discovery that they are out of duties of nature which harass them and delay them from achieving ultimate success immediately after schooling.

Truly, I would say that ***Ekeh Joe Obinna*** is a conquered mind indeed. I am yet to read your other book entitled ***Kingdom Far Away.***

Agoha Bob Ifeanyi
(Head, International Liaison & Outreach, The Electoral Institute, INEC, Nigeria)

INTRODUCTION

After Schooling is a practical guide written to elevate life of undergraduates, employees, unemployed youths, business men and women, and employers of labour. Its upbeat advice is focused on the journey of successful living. It is about creating a mindset of positive values that allow you to perceive your life as one of abundance, not as one of deficit. If you are an undergraduate, you may have realized that job market is not an ideal. Understand that job opportunity, by any means, is not the end of the trouble with life after schooling. No matter your present experiences, **after schooling**, only the strong-willed will **keep moving**.

Therefore this book prepares undergraduates, graduates, and business people for the real world with a positive mental attitude 'driven' from a negative mental attitude. However, it does not suggest that schooling is a waste of time, rather it teaches people 'why' and 'how' they should not be struggling with life or stuck in the wilderness of unemployment even with the rising number of unemployed youths in the country. Their minds will embrace the concept that the good opportunity in the land is unlimited. This means that they should not fear, and should not blame anybody should they become unsuccessful in their businesses, or remain employees till unnecessary number of years of lifelong.

After Schooling is not just concerned with financial education, although there is a great financial aspect that can be applied by today's business people, employers of labour, workers, or any money seeker. It offers people a practical counselling service, where financial success, job performance, entrepreneurship, and successful living are the issues. It is viewed as a tool that delivers the vital information every man on the journey of living success may seek.

Apparently, unemployment is a global crisis which is also resulting from insufficient job opportunity. It is an economic indicator which cannot be completely resolved. It all depends on how we view our personal circumstances, and changing it will help to change how we view our environment and the world at large. What matters after all is being successful. However, it is realizing that graduates have been 39.1% the cause of the rising number of unemployed youths in the country through their focus on what they do not need rather than putting their focus on what they do need. If you've just experienced heartache over this prospect, then this book is for you. The information in this book can reduce stress, increase your business's productivity, job performance, and give you the time needed to acquire a complete living success.

It is a book to put you under checks and balances as you grow in your quest for successful living. So I brought to you, youths, who are just starting and those who have already begun their journey of living success what I call PRACTICAL GUIDE and THE Twenty-two laws of enduring success to unlock your true potentials in walks of life, in order to meet ultimate success in your career and other relative areas of life. Do not stop reading, it's worth it. Because it contains the entire stimulus needed to prepare every normal mind with consciousness to attract one's desired life and become successful.

ONE

Concentrate Your Understanding

In the beginning, I know you have the ability to achieve success in life. I believe that was the purpose you enrolled for formal education to make it easier. Therefore, I urge you to give your attention to the knowledge that there are conditions which must be agreed about life before success can happen. There are no other physicians other than to demand of yourself determination, persistence, focus, commitment, and continuous effort as you step into the real world after schooling. To live continually in the application of unstoppable actions toward achieving your desired life is the only comforter to dissipate the shadows of unemployment and failure.

Until desire is developed, and be in harmony with your thoughts and actions, there is no intelligent accomplishment. Therefore, upon the task of thinking of the kind of person you desire to become, concentrate your thoughts and never stop trying as you have realized that there is no level of wealth or position that cannot be achieved if you have developed a certain level of unshakeable self-confidence.

As a young person, whosoever you become, whichever job you accept, including the wife or husband you marry in future is as a result of choices you make now you are young. Whatsoever your life unveiled to you in future cannot be different from the choices you're making now you are young. Always remember that those who have made wrong choices, those who have no central purpose, no defined desire fall a double times to petty worries and trials.

You are in a serious period of choice making in the ongoing journey of life and successful living. Success and failure are right in your hands; they are dwelling in your mind, in the constitution of your own thoughts and spoken words. Unfortunately, no one can be young twice to live a brand new life. It is clear you cannot return to tenth year of your life to make changes. But you can begin now to make a brand new management in the area of your dominant aspiration to achieve your desired life. Put it at the back of your mind that unemployment is not a reality. Youth-life is time to be deliberate and realistic with choice making. It holds a commanding foundation for entire future. It's a great privilege to be young. Many old people realize this and wish to become young again.

In the year 2012, after my engineering training, in School of Engineering, department of Mechanical Engineering of Institute of Management and Technology (IMT), Enugu, I was among those mobilized graduates for National Youth Service, and I was oriented at National Youth Service orientation camp Umudi, Imo State. After my twenty-one days of National Youth Service orientation course, I began to search for the justice that regulates the life of man, to discover the hidden possibilities and chances within man, and causes of his every condition. I have realized that one thing that doesn't make sense about life is that both wrong choices and right choices are irreversible. It is at your youth that you make the choice of foundation of what you want for your career and how to achieve your desired life. The proof of this statement is in the condition of life of every individual who has already gone on-board of the journey of real life and achieving success. As a reminder to yourself to follow certain instructions, it will be wise to also remind yourself that your success continues now.

I do not come to you, my brothers and sisters, with enticing words. I made up my mind to forget about everything but to bring this message to you. I declare this message to those who are mentally, spiritually, and physically matured. My wisdom does not belong to one of those gained from classroom lectures, but the secret of my wisdom is hidden from the majority of men and women. As for those who will embark on their one year national service, I want to wish you all good luck. Remember this day and the period of your National Service. It's more important than the time you were offered admission to continue schooling in order to obtain a degree or diploma certificate. But before you proceed, there is something you may need to know. Do not think you are special or that you can get luckier (of course you can), what I'm saying is, there is a backlog of graduates on a long queue awaiting employment. Above seventy percent of these potential graduates who have been certified with National Youth Service certificate are already complaining; and accusing Nigerian government for the schlock. As you already know, there is no job opportunity somewhere waiting for every Nigerian graduate, but there is a guaranteed career that can be developed in every Nigerian. Going to school is no longer sufficient. Begin now to radically alter your thoughts, to consider an alternative of what you could do to achieve your success and financial freedom if job opportunity did not come so fast. There is gold everywhere. Success is an affair of the mind. Your certificate is no longer a guarantee for job security and schooling does not truly guarantee financial success in life. Your life has just begun. Define your true self and the world will soften towards you.

This is the most crucial time of your life because it is the determinant equation of the rest of your life. As soon as you steps into the real world after schooling, all ways will change. Attractions will come. Challenges will come. Usually, inner crises will start within your mind, "I wish I was someone else," or "I wish my parents were rich." All these are what make life meaningful after graduation. Alter, as necessary, your basic understanding about real life when you step into the real world after schooling.

Family members, friends, including Nigerian government have interest in what you shall become after schooling. The trouble is, even when you are gainfully employed you may still find it difficult with financial matters, and to remain successful is based on your choices, decisions, and habits. Yet, put success as the only option. Failure has always been an effect of wrong thoughts and decisions in some direction. It is an indication that the individual is not in harmony with his being, his real man. It is a fate resulting from your choices, from the offspring of your thoughts. "It is in your moments of decision that your destiny is shaped." - Anthony Robbins. Put in your mind that nothing can stop the man with the right mental attitude from achieving his goal and nothing on earth can help the man with the wrong mental attitude. Keep away from people who always try to belittle your ambition. Most people always do that. They will bring up all the circumstances and try to make you see the difficulties in them. As your power is in your ability to decide, so is your financial success in your ability to govern your mind.

On a Tuesday evening, seven months after my National Youth Service, I was sitting outside my apartment with my certificate of National Youth Service and my school results beneath an office file on a small stool in front of me when my hand phone rang. It was my friend Mohamed Abdullahi calling. I gazed upon the wind. It had been long since he called me last. Abdullahi was a friend I met during my National Youth Service orientation course. I lowered my gaze when I noticed he was lamenting at the other end of the phone call. There was no job opportunity yet. He complained bitterly, rained curse on Nigerian leaders as he called them wicked politicians and mad dogs who knew only but the names of their banks and account numbers.

When he calmed down a little, I asked him the question I

had wanted to ask him.

"When you spoke to Emmanuel did he say he has gotten a job?

"Yes, he has gotten a job. He now works with Globacom Limited."

I could sense all the disappointment in Abdullahi's voice. So I remained where I was with my hand phone still connected and placed to my left ear. I was worried too. After a moment of silence, then, came Abdullahi's trembling voice again. But now, it was calm and he talked slowly; and somehow sounded as if he was going to cry.

"Please did you see the ADs on The Daily Sun today?" he asked me.

I knew I had not seen The Daily Sun newspaper for the day and I also knew he was not expecting me to answer him. He only needed me to reassure him that job opportunity would soon come. It was painful. I felt my mouth turned dry.

Abdullahi was not the only one who complained of unemployment. My cousin-brother studied economics and he came out with good grades. He had hurried across cities for screening exercises for a number of times. He also felt very bad each time he was not called for the job. My friend Olajumoke Josephine Akintunde dramatized on the shameful condition bitterly too, not once, not twice. In a sense, I became very worried. Acquiring good grades and multiple numbers of certificates is no longer sufficient for job security and nobody seems to have noticed, except about 25.7% of graduates. Undergraduates have not noticed that there is a problem with schooling. It neither secures automatic job for school leavers, nor does it prepares graduates for the real life with financial skills and basic principles of successful living should they become employers of labour, business people, or employees. It does only little but to provide graduates with certificates and leave them on their own to face the real world unprepared.

As I studied the issue of unemployment in Nigeria, I realized that the problem with unemployed graduates may be traced back to weak and wrong orientation given to them. A great percentage of today's graduates are not rightfully conditioned. It is a well known fact with plenty of evidence. Until graduates are gainfully oriented to conduct a harmonious adjustment of their inner man with their immediate surroundings, there is no successful living. Dismiss, also, the thoughts that the nature of unemployment will totally change in respect to government intervention. Surely, government have great role to play in downgrading the increasing rate of unemployment and they may have done little. But institutions of learning are the only buildings with tomorrow inside it, and they may have done nothing to prepare graduates for the real world.

I told a friend who studied Computer Engineering to get prepared. It should no longer be, "go to school, master your degree, and you could gain a high paying job", rather it should be "go to school, master your skills, acquire the required knowledge and you could run a higher paying job."

In the year 2005, I was offered admission to study Mechanical Engineering. During the new students' orientation programme, they told us that the orientation was designed to help us uncover the answers to the questions we had, and provide us with information about campus resources, programmes, and services. That, by the time we leave from the orientation ceremony, we will be on our way to becoming successful students. They did not tell us that after becoming successful students, we would float in the air as we looked for job opportunities, which we would have to queue alongside other unemployed graduates ahead of us. They did not tell us that there was no job security anymore.

They told us to make good grades. They told us that most times big companies would come for direct recruitment based on high-profile graded students. As we began schooling, we worked very hard to pass our exams. We did all manner of pernicious things. Most times, we bribed lecturers to stay above. We put all our efforts and minds to get high grades. We did not study to acquire knowledge, we read to pass only our exams. We followed the simple advice, "Do all you have to do to get high grades." They taught me Mechanical Engineering, taught my cousin-brother Economics, and taught Callista Maduekwe Accounting. But they neither taught me how to own a Mechanic Engineering Workshop, nor taught Callista Maduekwe how to begin to build her Accounting firm. They only oriented us for employment *after schooling*.

This orientation makes over sixty-eight percent of Nigerian graduates misunderstand the true nature of journey of life, living success, and the operation of their minds. They let it fill their minds with false contents. Yet, it leaves them detropped and unsuccessful after schooling. Because of this, schooling is no longer final. All ways have changed. Be not impatient to think, for being good is not just good enough any longer. Graduates should mentally set out on a straight pathway with conceived purpose. Most do not seem to understand that after schooling, to keep moving, they need to merchandise a positive interpersonal and intra-personal mentality to venture into the un-constructed narrow road to living success. Since the great global financial collapse and economic meltdown, the street has been the only entrepreneurial environment where being a successful student is not good enough. It is an entrepreneurial war zone where only the interpersonal and intra-personal intelligent people with positive mental attitudes survive. With a positive mental attitude, you meet the brighter side of life. You'll become optimistic and expect the best to happen. It is certainly a state of mind that is very well worth developing. There is no truth in the statement that opportunity comes knocking on the door only but once in a lifetime. The truth is that opportunity will never seek you, you seek opportunity. What usually turns out for a man's food usually turns out for another man's poison. When you say you "can", another man says he "can't", but he has not tried it yet. Understand that life will convey every man where he's heading to by the law of his own being. This law is made by character which has resulted from man's thought, which is in agreement with his choices. These choices will build-up man. It is true that government have roles to play to influence the overpowering wilderness of unemployment, but government have no role to play in deciding your living success after school. You alone have the power to determine that. Doubt and fear should be rigorously displaced. If you saw yourself through schooling, with all the environmental traits as they may had surfaced, then, you are already a potential man of success. Eleanor Roosevelt once says "No one can make you feel inferior without your consent." It is in your hands to choose. To move to success, you must make up your mind to move your mind. Everything man attains and all he fails to attain is as a result of his thoughts. Those who become successful and have acquired blessed wealth are not really those who leave the four walls of school with good grades, but they are those who utilize the ability they have. Not those who depend on paid job, but those who have given their singleness of purpose.

In 2012, a friend of mine called me into her apartment and she was crying bitterly. She sat on the floor and was tearing herself apart. As she cried, she mumbled, "What will I tell my husband?" I have never seen her in such a devastated condition. When I asked her what happened, she explained that she was not properly admitted into the university. For that reason, she was expelled from school; and she was a fourth year student on a five year course of study. I wondered why all that was happening to her. This was a very good friend of mine. Even when I told her it was okay, I knew it wasn't. But months later, I heard other stories. That she was mobilized for National Youth Service. When we spoke on telephone, she explained to me that her husband paid her way in. Hence she was pregnant, and gave birth during her service year. She had her National Youth Service certificate and she finally went home happily. She kept her certificate, she wasn't worried about job.

I understand that some thing could be a bargain to a certain degree. But the question is, "Was she studying to acquire certificate?" or "Was she studying acquire education? Most people are like that. They are after certificates instead of acquiring the basic education. They think they will become rich and be able to acquire assets once they're gainfully employed with highly graded certificates. They are right; yet they don't know that certificates will not make one successful. Only acquired skills and knowledge practically directed towards some worthy end will make one successful. Certificate represents nothing but miscellaneous guarantee and uncertain capacity and ability.

A true man of success does not think of what others think of. A true man of success may not directly choose his circumstances, but he can choose the way he wants to think about it, thereby shaping the demand of his every condition. Instead of criticising Nigerian system of government, you can analyse it. Analyse the events and the economic reasons that led to amalgamation of Northern Nigeria protectorate and Southern Nigeria protectorate by Sir Frederick Lugard in 1914 after he took office in 1912, which now leads the way for Nigeria to hold a commanding respect and power among all other African countries, in trading and in businesses. Do not look down on a country that presents and possesses unlimited opportunities and possibilities, including all the rights and freedom to acquire wealth and riches that may be required by any sincere mind. Nigeria is a great country with great people. Let failure find its false contents in another country. The wilderness of unemployment can cause social unrest which can also lead to revolution. Crisis arisen from National Immigration recruitment centres on 15th March, 2014 was a case in point. It cannot be completely resolved. It is as fateful as wanting to eradicate poverty. It can only be downgraded. Owing to growth in population and differences in thinking orientation, it will continue nagging as it recorded that unemployment rate in Nigeria had increased from 21.10% in 2010 to 23.90% in 2011 by National Bureau of Statistics.

It is no longer sufficient for employable graduates to sit at home thinking and waiting for government to resolve the issue of unemployment. Man is made to endure in purity of sincere answer to question such as 'what should I do next?' whenever he finds himself in a locked-down conditions. President Goodluck Ebele Jonathan, on Democracy Day, 29th May, 2012, addressed Nigerians with boldness when he says "*Fellow Nigerians, when I assumed office as acting President, in 2010, on account of the health challenges suffered by late President Umaru Musa Yar'Adua, there was so much anxiety in the land. The tone of public debate was febrile. Some persons sought to use the situation in the country to sow the seed of discord. There are challenges, yes, but we are working hard to address those challenges. And, by God's grace, we will succeed. My confidence is bolstered by the result which we have achieved in different sectors within the last twelve months.*

Today, I want to talk about what we are doing and what we have done. I want to reassure you that we are making progress. But, we can also do a lot more; and we must, and we will.

Many Nigerians were worried about the growing rate of unemployment. In order to set Nigeria on a sound and sustainable path toward economic growth, this unveiled a set of priority policies, programmes, and projects encapsulated in the Transformation Agenda. These programmes and policies are aimed at consolidating our budget, fostering job creation, engendering private sector-led inclusive growth, and creating an enabling environment for business to thrive for the ultimate betterment of the lives of Nigerians.

Today, progress has been made. The country's credit rating is positive, downgraded. In 2011, our foreign exchange reserves had risen to $37.02 billion, the highest level in 21 months. We have stabilized and improved our fiscal regime; we brought the fiscal deficit down to 2.85% of GDP from 2.9% in 2011. We reduced recurrent expenditures from 74% to 71% and reduced domestic borrowing from N852 billion in 2011 to N744 billion in 2012. We cut out over N100 billion of non-essential expenditure and increased our internally generated revenue from N200 billion to N467 billion.

For the first time over a decade, we now have a draft Trade Policy which provides a multidimensional framework to our trade regime and facilitate the inflow of investment. We have generated over N6.6 trillion works of investment commitments. The total value of our trade is also much higher than the value estimated in the previous year due to deliberate government policies.

Our goal is to ensure that every Nigerian can find gainful employment. Given my dissatisfaction with the prevailing unemployment situation in the country, we have embarked on an ambitious strategy of creating jobs and job-creators through the launch of several initiatives mainly targeted at the youths and women.

In October 2011, we launched the Youths Enterprise with Innovation in Nigerian programme, designed to encourage entrepreneurship and provide grants for small and medium scale enterprise. Over 1,200 Nigerians youths have benefited from this initiative. We have also launched the Public Works Women and Youths

Empowerment programme, which is designed to employ 370,000 youths per annum, with 30% of the jobs specially reserved for women.

*Let me make it clear here that our **You WIN** programme is designed to nurture and mentor young entrepreneurs to become major players, employers and wealth creators in business.*

We are gradually reducing the footprints of government in business activities through privatisation, liberalization and deregulation based on our recognition that the private sector should be the engine of growth in our economy."

He ended the Classic Speech saying *"The Federal Government will also establish an Institute of Democracy Studies and Governance in the universities."* - President Goodluck Ebele Jonathan's Address, May 29, 2012.

Mr. President has not failed us. Nigerian government has not completely succeeded in addressing the issue of unemployment that is threatening the life of most school leavers and the peace of mind of most of our dear parents. The truth is that they will only have to continue working on it while we keep increasing in population with different thinking orientations. In few months from now, another set of corps members would emerge from National Youth Service. And to think that the majority of orientation camps in the country recruit not less than two thousand, five hundred candidates, and sometimes above, with only few of these orientation camps recruiting lesser. This means we should expect not less than eighty-five thousand graduates and above every five months to join the labour market.

Every Nigerian graduate should wake up. Nigeria provides all the freedom and opportunity to become financially successful that any sincere person may require.

When one goes farming, one selects the kind of farming tools and island where one's crops may grow healthy and in abundance. And one is obligated to protect the crops till a lasting time. When seeking financial success and wealth, the same rule is required. Think twice, you, graduates and unemployed youths who are truly seeking job opportunity and financial freedom before trying to destroy the minds of youths whose annual expenditure on internet subscription runs into hundreds of millions of naira; with the bulk of the income going to three major telecommunication companies only. Think twice, you, youths, parents, leaders before trying to condemn the economic capitalistic system of a country whose domestic borrowing was N744 billion naira only (2012), and internally generated revenue upgraded to about N467 billion naira. Please give plenty considerations and do not destroy the economic balance of a country who does not tax her citizens (both citizen by birth, citizen by registration, citizen by naturalization or otherwise) to death. Wrong information should be sincerely displaced. Many Nigerians are gainfully employed and many are already employers of labour, but the problem is mismanagement of funds which they do not teach its fundamental knowledge in school. While some have also refused to seek that knowledge which is the only dependable way to cultivate and develop a true mind that is ready to attract riches and catapult one from one's present adversity to one's highest station. A country like Nigeria where one has full right and freedom to accumulate wealth and riches to any possible height without restriction from government is a country to consider, heartily.

The road to success is very narrow. And after the journey of life, the successful number is just few. Do not be afraid; and do not make the mistake of thinking that Nigeria is a wrong choice when acquiring wealth and riches are the issues. There are many people who have made their success in one business idea or the other. These are people who understood, and have obeyed the ***basic law of prosperity*** mandated to man. You can follow in their footsteps and achieve your own financial success in any business endeavour. Most people may not be able to state clearly what they want most in life when you ask them. While some will say it's gainful employment, others will simply tell you money, good cars, good houses, but no one is ready to plant the seed of prosperity while life lasts. Unemployment is a reproach after schooling. It should be fact of a number of unemployable people not having talents, jobs, or businesses. They somehow have no love for majority of things that happen around them. They are the total number of unemployable people owing to wrong orientation. In an attempt to address this issue rising from the wilderness of unemployment, Minister of Finance and Coordinating Minister of the Economy, Dr. Ngozi Okonjo Iweala while commissioning the Global Distance Learning Institute, GDNL, in Abuja said that efforts would be made to encourage unemployed youths in the country to become entrepreneurs and employers of labour; saying that there were over 5.3 million backlog of unemployed youths and about 1.8 million graduates enter the job market every year. "We feel what the youths are feeling and if we have 1.8 million unemployed youths and we create 1.6 million jobs, it gives hope." The Vanguard 4th April, 2014- pg 15. Creativity seems to be the only one left in the world of job creation.

Somewhere in our makeup, we blame our leaders. Maybe they put us in the last category of their list of schedule. Maybe it is no longer fatal for the nation to over look the urgency of the matter. It's all right because I know they are trying and they will continue to try a lot more. But, there will neither be rest nor tranquillity in the nation until school leavers are granted the required sensitization. The wilderness of unemployment will continue to shake the foundation of the nation and the world at large until a bright day of real education emerges. In a future not so far, there will come a time when employees and unemployed youths will begin to discover the possibility of achieving their financial freedom and living success. That period is dawning like a long darkest night. There is no longer delay. A woman in her late pregnancy may suffer labour pains, but when the time is due for the baby to be born, there is no longer delay. That same way, it will manifest. The whole job markets will be filled with masters in practical knowledge allied with financial skills and basic principles of living success. Masters who will rather choose to venture into self-oriented business ideas. Any one who is employed will be regarded as uneducated man who has no required knowledge. **Wrong Orientation, Omission of Financial Education, and Lack of the Knowledge of the Basic Principles of Successful Living** paralyse the hand-wheel of labour market. Out of experiences of unemployment and failure will raise and stand leaders in entrepreneurs and employers of labour who will observe and obey the commandment of success. These leaders will come from the business histories of common employees and unemployed youths who now suffer the fate of unemployment and failure, and will sooner or later develop from within. And others who now labour in bank industries, factories, other production companies, and so on.

School system is due for a complete reform. Do not misunderstand me about this. The system of the past should go with the past. It is no longer sufficient to go through the tunnel expecting to see a light. It's about time you carry your lamp along. It's about time Financial Education and Basic Principles of Success are introduced to undergraduates and potential graduates. If you're one of those whose financial success is long overdue, probably, you've waited for job opportunity and it hasn't come, or you're one of those suffering in the wilderness of wrong employment, is you delay due to possible financial illiteracy? Are you struggling with financial issues and life seems to have remained static? Are you in business and yet there is no trace of financial freedom upfront? Do not doubt that a man can acquire knowledge to **keep moving** to a successful living. Man can see himself rise to his highest station after school by the laws he obeys. Nature already has a habit of making rooms for success for the man whose words and actions show he knows where he is heading to. With more or little schooling, always remember that ideas **'make'** and **'rule'** the world. Your journey to financial success after school can be as simple as having fun with what you love doing always. But, no matter what you love doing, there are certain elements most likely needed to be present for you to achieve ultimate financial success. These elements are not taught in institutions of higher learning nationwide.

You will need to understand and develop your own winning ways when you discover your **passion**. Have faith, take responsibility, and think positively. You will need to take actions, embrace the pains of your setback when they come. Study while others are sleeping, work while others are loafing, prepare while others are playing. Those who have acquired perpetual things worth having in this life have invested while others idled their funds. They have persevered while others gave up in despair. They have practised the valuable habits of self-denial, industry, and singleness of purpose. Finally, having mentors, confronting and resolving obstacles, helping others, recognizing opportunities and refusing to quit will galvanise you in your quest for financial freedom, and also make you a **co-creator**. If going to school can help somebody acquire potential knowledge, then simple application of the basic principles described in this book will propel you to becoming successful.

Two

Keep Moving

Man is born and equipped to succeed, not to fear and fail. But unfortunately, most graduates do not understand the overriding power of their own personal willpower. Remove failure as an option. The potentials you seem to have acquired from formal education are not necessarily what you may need. Beyond the knowledge you have acquired, on the journey of successful living, friends, parents, environments, peers will help to keep you moving. Your task is not to allow others to wrongly shape your personality for you. The solution to moving forward with or without a monthly paid job is a form of retreat inside you. When you realize this, you will begin to control your thoughts, regulate, and discipline your mind, and rebuild the inner state of your soul by eliminating all the wrong materials to incorporate into your being the necessary elements to keep moving from achieving success throughout your schooling to becoming successful after schooling. You don't need to work harder than you should in the area of your dominant aspiration if your notion is moulded and shaped to suit your immediate condition. Working harder is an old idea which was born in the olden days of no education. Understand that man is a free agent. He only has to ***desire, think***, and ***plan*** well. "One step - choosing a goal and sticking to it - changes everything." - Scott Reed. This commandment was made by nature which described that desire is the only starting point of all achievements. Keep this in mind always.

Owing to preconceived notions, most graduates have refused to merchandise enough courage and self-confidence. They do not think they can simply become successful in any business endeavour of their own. They seem to be conquered by fear of failure more than they want to enjoy success. Hence I tell you, Nigerian environments are too fertile. Maybe you have learned things from others. Most times, these things aren't based on facts and may even prove to be incorrect. They could have been only opinions, but you learnt them as truths and they cause fear that keeps you from pursuing your dreams.

Example: Your fear for financial success and successful living may be because you grew up hearing and believing that Nigeria is not good enough for business ideas, you may wish to leave the country, or you may have heard that Nigerian system of government has not provided sufficient infrastructures for business opportunities and you have believed it. Every time you meet an unsuccessful graduate, it validates this belief. Your fear of moving on overcomes your desire for financial freedom. Now, when all your doubts, fears, and insecurities get your attention, you usually come up with the idea of "I wish I was somebody else", or "I wish my parents were rich." More often than not, you think and believe that it's better to get employed and stay employed. While in reality, your employer knows you have potentials which is why he employed you. He needs your service to survive his business. He is just using your knowledge and skills to achieve his own financial freedom. He adopts the law of economics: when you become more professional, he pays you higher and leaves more perpetual responsibilities in your command. And then, life challenges come up to your neck. He keeps you away from real life; from knowing how to bargain with life on your own and start achieving a living success through a defined dream. Success does not end in having a job. The journey of successful living begins after schooling and continues throughout the years of employment or business adventures, and then endures after it.

I read on The Nation Newspaper dated 5th Feb, 2013, about workers of a South-Korean firm, SOPHIA MANUFACTURING LIMITED, makers of Xpression brand of hair extensions, of over 200 workers protesting against poor condition of service and welfare packages. They demanded salary increment, which they said was long overdue. They carried placards with inscription like, "exploitation must stop in Sophia", "no N7, 500.00, no work," and "salary increment is our right", and among others. They blamed their plights on government's insensitivity to the welfare of the youths, lamenting that there were not enough employment opportunities for school leavers. *"If government had created enough employment opportunities for us youths, the Koreans would not be exploiting us the way they are doing because there would have been many options available to school leavers. We have worked here for over five years, yet, housing, transport, and food are increasing by the day."*

I took out a deep breath as I folded the newspaper; and then there were growing pains all over my body. Employees are suffering, and most people's own get worse. No employer/company pays employees up to sixty-five percent of what they lose working for them. "In an interview with the Minister of Power, Prof. Chinedu Nebo during the privatization of Power Holding Company of Nigeria after it handed Company over to the ten successor companies, it was recorded that only about forty percent of the old workforce in process was retained, while sixty percent others were handed disengagement letters. It was about 47,000 workers of the defunct PHCN who received disengagement letters from Federal Government of Nigeria."- The Punch, 5th May, 2014. This is response to civilization from capitalistic Nigeria. I am not attempting to beef Nigeria system of economic development, nor do I attempt to condemn the achievement of the disengaged workers. I only intend to express the opinion that job opportunity is an affair of the head; entrepreneurship is that of the mind. As long as civilization demands, many will lose their jobs and only fewer than expected will be employed. The rest will dedicate to one business, trading, or the other, while employable graduates will resolve and keep moving to become entrepreneurs.

After Schooling, no matter how trivial life without a monthly paid job is, one should also understand that job opportunity is not the only significant rival to successful living. My parents may have worked for a company for little pay and job benefits because they did not think like I do. I was born into the rapidly changing world which has originated different circumstances and I see things differently. If I, **Ekeh Joe Obinna**, am thinking like everyone else, then I'm not thinking. My thoughts are those of a successful master. Would I have worked with a company, and continued working with the company not to have my own company? I'm sure most graduates have the same wishes as I do. I hope that what I'm doing now will determine where I would be in some time to come. I also know that it is not a simple matter to become successful in life, and also get everything I want. So I will try my best to make this a reality. I have always asked myself what I actually want in life, why I live here on earth, and why did I enrol for formal education. I'm sure it's to become successful and aid others to succeed too. Although in hard times I felt like I would have to commit one crime or the other to keep moving in life. And if I had turned into a criminal, I would have been the world most wanted for turning intelligence into impurity. But I understand that no pure minded man would turn into a criminal by mere external forces of physical living. It is interestingly important to **desire, think,** and **plan** very well. I will also have to be courageous, strong, and prepared to face every setback that would always come.

One late morning, I was sitting on my desk in my bedroom, writing my second novel when a friend of mine came to my house with an infected mind. He was concerned with financial job. He complained his savings has gone down. He had spent about 24 percent of his savings, which left him with only seventy-eight thousand, six hundred naira. He was afraid he might spend the remaining fund in time to come. He pleaded we should put heads together to come up with a business idea. I have heard people say Nigeria have few or insufficient infrastructure, I have also seen people complain of Nigeria having ill-security grade. But, I did not see where that may affect the business idea I discovered. I used my power of imagination to mould and create a definite job that suited his personality. Albert Einstein says "I am enough of an artist to draw freely upon my imagination. Imagination is more important than undirected knowledge. Undirected knowledge is limited. Imagination encircles the world."

It was at night when I was relaxing in my bedroom, in my bed, going through my book that an idea popped into my head. I had read in a book that everything man imagined was real. So the next day, I called him to analyze the new discovery. I called it **Financial Agency**. It was a lucrative virgin business idea. All he had to do was to dress cooperate in starched shirt and well ironed trouser. He did not have to look bad. He had an identity card that set his name as a financial agent. He took alongside a laptop computer which he used to log into the internet. That same courage carried him into the market premises. He said traders were amazed and stunned as he introduced himself as a financial agent. They never heard of it in that manner.

Some traders decided to try his service. As a financial agent, his job was to help traders to pay in money into their bank accounts or their customers' bank accounts. But, he did not have to go from bank to bank to pay in the money. He collected the money from them and made fund transfer from his own bank account to the beneficiary bank account, with little interest of N200 depending on the amount he transferred and the beneficiary bank. Afterwards, he moved to the next shop to look for other interested clients. It was a marketable business idea, very lucrative. Today, he's grateful that traders would not want to risk going to banks to deposit funds on a daily basis. He makes not less than seventy-five transfers in a week (six market days).

Everything man can imagine is real. Man is poor only if he chooses to be poor in thinking. Unemployment is a state of the mind. What I discovered is how to use the issue of insecurity to regulate the fate of unemployment because I believe there is ability in disability. It is your choice to choose which one you want to nurture in your mind. Success comes to those who constantly think in terms of '*I can*', '*I will*, and '*I am*'. But failures concentrate their waking thoughts on what they should have or would have done, or what they can't do. This lucrative business idea has benefitted only four individuals owing to the delay in publication of this book. And considering my own analysis on the business idea, it can generate about twenty thousand naira or more in a week. It all depends on how many clients you can secure to yourself. You too can benefit from this business idea because the system and condition of societal environments elevate it. It saves the traders time and eradicates the risk and stress of going to bank for them. My friend started with limited capital of seventy thousand naira only. Anyone can start with liquid capital as low as fifty thousand naira. It depends on your target and how much you can, and wishes to stake, and then you can start immediately. "A man with courage is **majority**." - Andrew Jackson.

The secret of ultimate living is securely attached to the ability to keep moving after schooling, when job opportunity did not come so fast and you do not limit your willpower. When you can move on without having to force people or deceive them of their valuables, or simply hurt them. While you can do this without falling among other graduates who may have used up their savings while waiting for employment opportunity because they buy things they do not really need, to impress people they do not really know. They scan the internet and newspapers looking for job vacancies. Finally, they find one and submit their CVs and cover letters. And then, they go home to spend the rest of the day on Facebook, Twitter, Whatsapp, 2go, Instagram, Badoo, Pinterest, and other social networks. They don't really understand that if a job opportunity is on the front page of a newspaper, it is already late in most instances. It is meant for the masses.

You must wake up. Fashion weapon from what nature provides. The moment you stop trying to become a better person is the moment you start becoming worse than what you already are. You must keep moving. If you're going through hell, keep going because man does not live by bread alone. You must get to challenge yourself and look for an opportunity to try new things, and succeed in those new things. It is with this kind of open mind and thirst for intellectual adventure that you will discover and push the limit of your true potential.

When my cousin became hopelessly in debt, I did not only help him hock few of his property, but I also went into research to look for a business idea that would suit his personality. When I asked him what his desire was, he just replied, "I don't know." He studied economics and it was not his dreamed course of study, he explained. There made reasons for him to rest securely on seeking paid job opportunity. Most graduates share the same fate. They did not get to study their dreamed course. And now, they are afraid they would not get to their dreamed destination. They think they only need the job opportunity which their certificates can secure. Have you been misinterpreting some of these experiences negatively and they validate your fear? It is no longer a problem. Keep your mind alert and I will explain why and how it would no longer be a problem. This book will expand your view and bring out more willpower in you that will quicken your receptive desires and place it at your command for your own benefit. Do not spend a night alone. Keep on thinking on what you love doing until you fall asleep. I can tell you that '**love**' does not die, but it can fade or grow. I may be able to have the call of inspired preaching, but if I do not have love for people who I am called to preach and write to, then there is no success. David Frost, a British Journalist and Media Personality observed how eternal, kind, and patient love is when he says "Do what you're passionate about, no matter what it is." Find the way it works for you and keep doing it that way. Follow the Basic Principles of Success, and do not measure your success with other business initiators who are already successful in their business ideas. When you discover what you love doing, you will enjoy the time and strength you spend doing them. If your current profession is not one of your dreams, then consider bringing in your hobbies and talents into your work life. You can build a successful career around your beloved talents or hobbies; and you'll enjoy your work considerably. Only then will achieving success be as easy as having fun.

In the year 2010, when I wrote the first sentences of my novel entitled ***Kingdom Far Away***, I had no idea that those

35,323 word counts would change my life. I thought I was doing nothing more than reflecting on the knowledge I had attained in life; sharing a bit of what I had learned in life in a piece of writing. I thought it would be buried there inside my 13inch laptop's hard disk. I didn't imagine that in less than one year I would have a number of printed copies of my work in my bedroom. I didn't imagine I would have such number of schools to sell to. I didn't imagine my success would come this quick in the beginning. I was grateful. I didn't imagine that I would finally be out of debts, that I would have my second book demanded before I would get to publish it; that I would happily hand down my National Youth Service certificate and other certificates. At the end, my mind was made stronger by the aid of Almighty God.

It was an amazing realization that sometimes one rules out the possibility of a great change because it doesn't seem realistic to him. For nearly six years, I focused on going to higher institution, studying mechanical engineering. It was a great experience; all was good. I enjoyed my study. It is my **desire** to practice mechanical engineering, yet I have **passion** for creative writing too.

In an interview I was asked, "*Was writing on your mind while growing up?*"

I simply took out a deep breath and answered. "*Yes, writing was on my mind, but being a novelist was certainly not my aim.*" I could remember that my greatest moments were the times I enjoyed reading books. When I would sit alone and write down episodes of life experiences. I didn't write to impress a certain religion, denomination, nation, or people. I only wrote for divine; to express the great message and secret truths through creativity, by the power of the Spirit, to give myself help, encouragement, and comfort. And also find people who it appeals to.

Even though you may not have a complete sense of how what you desire to do will fit into the big scheme of things, if you love it and think it's right for you to do, just do it. "Never be afraid to tread on the path alone. Know which one is your path and follow it to wherever it may lead you. Do not feel you have to follow in someone else's footsteps." - Eileen Caddy. Success comes to the man who will use his skills and constructive imaginations to see what he can do to succeed, instead of what people want him do.

One Saturday morning, I and my friends were discussing about business ideas after morning jogging at stadium. Charles pulled all stunts and stubbornness as he refused to accept that most of the business ideas will flourish in the land. He was so terrified at not accepting that Nigeria could be fruitful in running business ideas. I simply put it that people who have low self-esteem cannot attain financial success. Charles was, as well, sustained by his monthly income, and his late father owned a bungalow where his family lived. He complained of Nigeria lapses. He worked with a fast food company as a technical supervisor where they paid him thirty thousand naira monthly, and it was fine by him as he said. They had standby power generator at home and water supply system that fed the whole building. So, he seemed comfortable. But he couldn't recognize an opportunity that stared right at his face. His anger couldn't let him think; his emotion was thinking for him.

A football rolled over to our side and Israel kicked the ball and it landed on a big constructed iron water tank that supplied water in the stadium. I stared at him, then, back at the tank. Israel thought it was the noise. I just recognized a business idea. I could remember neighbours coming to Charles' house most times to beg for water. I told Charles he could actually run a waterworks business. I know Nigeria does not restrict that idea. Israel said it was not possible, that it was very expensive. He said that Charles would run out of money from buying gas and maintenance; that there was poor power supply and electric power charge rate was also expensive. But Charles did not talk. He seemed to be thinking about it. At evening, I and Charles did all the analysis and it was a little bit approachable. We decided we should write a proposal to about six neighbouring buildings and see their responses. Few days later, Charles called me to tell me that only two buildings out of the six buildings we proposed to supply water responded positively. Charles went ahead to running the business contract. Those houses bought their overhead water tanks and Charles called his plumber who fixed his water-system for his late father and the plumber installed the water tanks.

It was only two buildings, so Charles only had to supply water to them in the morning before leaving to his place of work, and at evening when he returned from his workplace. Life is not meant to be struggled with, neither for. The problem with unemployment is of unemployment.

After about two months, Charles received a letter of proposal to run installation estimate for the third building. He had to install an external water pump, and also had to employ a secondary school teenager whose job was to come after school, to supply water to his clients at 4pm and buy gas for power generator. Charles was a Mechanic Engineer, and he worked as a technical supervisor so he covered that area of supervising his waterworks.

One thing I didn't imagine was that Charles would, at last, supply water to about eleven buildings, of which the smallest of the buildings was a building of four bedrooms flat which generated twenty-eight thousand, eight hundred naira only every six months. This means that the rest of the buildings generated, for Charles, an approximately income of about three hundred and ninety-six thousand naira every six months, after balancing his expenses from paying his employee and purchasing of gas. He had about fifty thousand, one hundred naira to build to his savings after the end of every month without having to touch his monthly salary at his workplace too.

Opportunity may not necessarily means what comes to you. You may have to consider what you can visualize, understand, and go after. One of the main weaknesses facing the majority of graduates is the average understanding of man that opportunity comes around. Opportunity does not **come** around, it has **been** around. It is about time to hit the bullet against inadequate knowledge. Let's remember who we are and try manifesting in our lives, in our own ways first. Think about how many times before now you have wished for something that came to pass. Your desire, your emotions, and the positive energies you emitted were what manifested those wishes. It was because on some level, you believed you could. Doing the best you can, with the little you have, is the only dependable starting point by which a permanent prosperity can be secured and endured. People who are poor simply have poor habits in wishing and in spending. This does not mean to say you should not cut down your expenses. It aims to express that the beginning of a glorious achievement starts with the understanding of the nature of the desire and the ability to spend all the required resources to achieve success in that desire.

"Anything in life worth having is worth working for" Andrew Carnegie. Failure is not an option. The problem with schooling is that majority of graduates often want to practice what they study in school with big companies.

When Anthony, my cousin, who studied economics, could not find a good job, he went for loan, but there was no trace of good financial position so the loan was not granted. He had to sell some of his property, including his laptop to boost his capital for a business idea we spent only two months to investigate and analyze. I specialize in machine design and construction, so I did the designing and construction of an incubator with limited capacity of two hundred and fifty eggs. His job was to visit poultry farm to source fresh fertilized eggs every seven days. After the construction of the incubator, he had only seventeen thousand naira left from the total money he realized from hocking his property. So he bought the first batch of eggs at one thousand, nine hundred and fifty naira only. Then after seven days, he bought another set of sixty fertilized eggs. During the incubating processes, he lost fourteen eggs. It was a great loss to him, so he stopped being disobedient man in school of his business experiences. He began to learn about it after he lost another twenty-one chickens owing to cold weather, and was left with only twenty-five chickens from the first sets of sixty eggs he incubated. He had not learnt, with humility and patience, his lessons on how to handle day-old chickens. So he went to library, scanned the internet, looked for books that dealt on that topic. Before the next sets of chickens were hatched, he was already professional awaiting the chickens. "Shoot for the moon; even if you miss, you will land among the stars." Less Brown.

Anthony has acquired two incubators. He processes about one hundred and eighty eggs weekly from the incubating machines. He would feed the survivals for another seven days and sell them at a higher price of three hundred and twenty naira (N320.00k) each.

After balancing his expenses from the cost of eggs, feeding them for seven days, and the medicine he puts in their drinking water, including miscellaneous expenses which he budgeted at ten percent, he had about forty-three thousand, seven hundred and eight naira (N43,780) every week.

Think twice, you, who have not investigated this business idea before condemning a lucrative business idea that lots of rich men and women who have acquired blessed wealth depend on. Now, Anthony has limited resources and capacity to accommodate the chickens for more than seven days because of the incubating eggs that will soon be due; and his clients book the chickens before the due dates.

We all have to keep moving. Most of the graduates and undergraduates have great run-ways already built for them. If you have one build for you, take off and keep moving to your own dominant aspiration. But, if you do not have any one yet, it is your responsibility to grab a shovel and build one for yourself, and for those who will follow after you.

I feel worried every time I hear someone say to me that he does not know what to do. That government has not provided sufficient infrastructures. That the roads in the country are not too good for him to venture into his business idea, or that there is no enough power supply. And I have always questioned such a person, "***Have you really defined your desire?***"

And a friend of mine, a law graduate, simply told me "I don't need all these knowledge. All I want is to become successful."

It is a common wish for most people. I am also not unmindful that what is good for a bus driver and a bus conductor is also good for the passengers. But every passenger has his own worth for his own destination. Every passenger will need to disclose his destination to hear his own price for his transportation ticket.

What is your desire?....it's achievable.

Three

Define Your Desire

Every young man who reaches the stage of understanding the purpose of money wishes to be financially successful. But wishes do not bring riches. Put in mind that it is one thing to desire something and another thing to walk through the right path towards achieving it. Sometimes, it is difficult for some people to define their true desires. That is why the majority of Nigerian graduates who await employment do not actually understand that their true wishes is to become successful, not just to be gainfully employed. Most of them relax, with certain thought that they have become successful, when they gain employment. They don't know that they actually need to work harder to remain employed and improve on their job careers towards achieving successful living.

This idea of wanting and seeking only the benefits of job opportunity was breast fed to stupor a little more than eleven years ago by a very wealthy business man. This billionaire was the one who invested millions of naira in multinational business opportunities. He was the owner of "Fast and Slow". A group of companies that dealt in poultry farming, book publishing, paint production, plastic industrialization, waste recycling and management, birds feeds' production, estate management, hospitals, production of school chalks, and so on. It had about one million and above in number of employees all over the nation, and beyond.

While the billionaire was on the journey of successful living, he suffered three heavy heart attacks in less than five years from overwork. He had sons who were doctors, but he had always felt that God had visited a curse on him as his sons could not source a lasting solution to his sickness.

I saw the billionaire twenty-four months ago, before I went for National Youth Service. He was in his bedroom, in his bed, when he phoned my friend who was a practicing doctor to come over. So, I went with my doctor-friend to the billionaire's house. The doctor examined him and assured him that the pains would go away. The doctor told him there was no problem, that the trouble was not too dangerous; that he should let himself fall asleep. The doctor measured his heartbeat with stethoscope, it was ok and intact.

I was sitting on a side chair when the billionaire stood to his feet. He was somehow naked without a long black garment, and he appeared very weak and troubled, but he was not yet finished. He staggered a number of times as he tried to walk over to the next chair. His veins on his neck showed clearly. His check bones pushed out, giving the impression of the hollow of his eyes sockets, like one who used methamphetamine. His head was bigger, and his skin looked spotty and drained from lack of good food nutrients. But this was a very wealthy business man.

I noticed that his clothes were dirty from two days of sweat, and it made him look like someone who slept on the street. Truly, things were not normal with him. He was rich. A lot of oil business moguls, politicians, including many foreign investors worshiped in his shrine. They drank from his cup. He owned hospitals with highly graded doctors who specialized in, and could handle all kinds of health challenges, yet they were unable to trace, and source a lasting solution to the billionaire's health challenges.

All along, till date, they are treating ulcer instead of heart failure. After few examinations on him, the doctor wrote a report with inscription of the billionaire's name behind the brown big envelope. His name is **_Mr. Institution of Higher Learning_**.

Institutions of higher learning are unhealthy. Hence they are treating ulcer while they're affected with heart failure. The primary role of learning institutions is to prepare undergraduates for future demands, as response to call of civilization. But there are also instances where corps members were observed to be unfit to even take up teaching appointments in secondary schools. This is the crown of the efforts installed in most graduates by most institutions of higher learning. But making sure that every young Nigerian receives quality **schooling** is an urgent need. Yet we realize that this cannot be achieved overnight. Every young Nigerian needs a clear vision of where he wants to be after schooling. And we must make sure that every period he moves a bit closer to his vision, with certain knowledge that a huge achievement is an accumulation of many smaller successes.

It is not going to remain the same. Learners must receive the training they require and paid for. And lecturers should understand the importance of their profession for the development of the nation and reducing of unemployment and do their utmost to give their learners a complete schooling and good education for the so purpose of meeting their desired lives after schooling.

The Deputy Governor of Central Bank of Nigeria (CBN), Tunde Lemo, on a convocation lecture, expressed the same observation when he says "It has become quite evident that very many modern day Nigerian graduates are not employable. The Nigerian educational system, particularly at the tertiary level, is bedevilled by myriads of problems ranging from poor funding, undue interference, outdated curricular, poor staffing, overcrowding and managements' incompetence." - Daily Independent, Oct 2, 2013.

All ways have changed. By the aid of pure reasoning, understanding, self control, righteousness, and well directed creative thoughts, graduates should ascend. Such is the true demand mandated to every Nigerian graduate. Until **financial skills** and **basic principles of successful living** are taught in all institutions of higher learning, and expressed the opinion that it should be attached to every course of study as a one year **finance** and **success** orientation course, and allow it to revolutionize the entire system of education, employable graduates will rather not understand how to dedicate to start resolving on their own. This opinion is made to increase the quality and value of Nigerian graduates, and also to double the respect of Nigerian employees. And only when considered, the wilderness of unemployment will not be brought to least minimum.

I have experienced that the courses which are taught in

institutions of higher learning are not truly a waste of time, but have only too little, whatsoever to applying the principles of successful living, business intelligence, interpersonal intelligence and intra-personal intelligence in real life. Should any graduate resolve to develop from within, to become an employer of labour, his setback becomes his inability to acquire financial intelligence and the knowledge of the basic principles of success while he was in school. These courses and the system of scheme of works in institutions of higher learning have rather no real value to an unemployed youth where financial literacy and enhanced skills are the matter. It leaves them in dry hands of real life challenges unaware and unprepared, and hence, strangles their dreams out of them. Another Author wrote: "*They Don't Teach Cooperate in College*" Alexandra Levit; a former nationally syndicated columnist for the Wall Street Journal, and a current writer for the New York Times. It is the same expression of how amazing it is, of what ordinary graduates can do if they set out without preconceived notions. It is the same expression that schools have not accepted responsibilities for changing conditions as they exist, but have only accepted conditions as they exist. Educators are working very hard to educate the students.

Yet, as far as schooling is concerned, those who master only in formal education work harder than they should because there is no true knowledge of principles of success, nor is there any presence of financial skills, and applying the principles of success looks abrupt as they are limited to unaware challenges of life and also by lack of adequate knowledge on how to establish in the courses which they have studied in school. And this has made the job opportunity of most employees their greatest achievement in life. They don't seem to understand life as they can't seem to bargain with life on their own terms.

It is a mandate given to man not to let his education interfere with his schooling. Most people who are now stuck in the fate of unemployment want a breakthrough. But they can't really seem to get traction. Contrary to what they think, it is not about having:
* More money or maybe, getting well paid,
* More time or maybe, working when you choose to,
* The right contacts or maybe, knowing the high-profiles, and
* Strong financial background.

Instead, it's always about having something to work for, and overcoming an invisible barrier that sincerely exist within your mind. The barrier is not something external. It is something internal something you have conceived in your own mind that is all right with you, in joy and in happiness. It is your *desire*, which was the main purpose you were sent into the world, and went through school to make it easier to achieve.

Herein, you can neither be replaced nor can your life be

repeated. Therefore, everyone's desire is as unique as his specific opportunity to attain it. Whether you're an employee or an entrepreneur, you are right. But put it in your mind that in twenty-five years from now you will be more disappointed by things that you didn't do than things you did. For if you choose not to retire at the age of fifty or fifty-five because you have been unable to put investments together to continue when after your retirement, then you should be, and would be counted among failures. There is no commandment of prosperity that man cannot keep. Unemployment is not truly a reality. Failure isn't too.

Some people still engage in the act of doubting that every man has his own specific vocation or mission in life. These are the percentage of people who have refused to understand that nature has not promised anyone something for nothing. Only you can, and will implement your own mission. This is one of the most wonderful and exciting facts about every man's life. There is a desire every man generates uniquely within him, and when he properly defines this desire, he will have the keys to unlock all other potentials in his life. The right achievement of this desire will result in happiness, satisfaction, fulfilment, good health, and so much more. There will be job opportunity or business, or sometimes both of them, when man generates the right desire. Only when this desire is properly defined, and man's actions are in harmony with the commandment of attaining it, will wealth and riches will be easily attained. And no environmental traits can boldly stop him. It doesn't matter if some people are laughing behind your back. Maybe they will be glad to see you fail. They laugh in your face while pretending to be your friend. Beware that things which you have not prepared for will happen but success can only be achieved when man generates to the right desire. That is, he has purified his mind to develop love for things and also passion for doing them. Man is obligated to dream of achieving his own desire. He must set his own standards to enable him to aim at his own goals and determine how to accomplish them.

One of the reasons why most unemployed youths cannot achieve their desired lives is because they place in their minds that employment is the only true way to get started. Hence they are not yet employed they fail within their minds. Then they blame friends, family members, leaders and environment for their failures. We can best understand what happen in the long run when an employee fails to liquidate from his employer, which expresses the fact that an employee without desire to accomplish is already a failure, for he will work for the rest of his life getting paid.

Achieving your desire is not about being job opportune ***after schooling***. So when there is no job, it's your wish that you ***keep moving***. When you define your own desire and believe in yourself and make a total commitment to your desire, and stake your materials, including your natural weapon into achieving it- your mind, your body, your heart and your spirit, only then will you experience the magnitude of a living success.

The truth of this statement is in the life of Bukky Bello who studied biochemistry in the University of Westminster, and today, she is into the business of creativity. She uses local contents to decorate and design a lot of things. It is a perfect love seeing its way through the mind of a successful virtue.

In an interview with Vanguard Newspapers, 16th March, 2014; she simply said "Ballafricana came as a result of my passion. Ever since I was young, I have always had passion for creativity. Whenever my parents asked me what I really wanted to do, I have always replied to them, interior decoration, because I love aesthetics and I am always curious as to how things came about."

Bellafricana is a business idea that is focused in promoting local content through producing gift items, corporate, promotional items, souvenirs, interior decoration and office, and casual wears in African textile.

What drove my passion the most was when she said "I rejected employment to create jobs with African textile." She had returned from United Kingdom after schooling to be here in Nigeria which she identified as fruition. Bellafricana has clients, and has supplied to companies both in Nigeria and the United Kingdom. Some of the company's items include: Notepad casing item, iPod casing items, pen pots items, cheque-book holders, shopping bag designed in African textiles, and many more items.

Any one with courage and passion can still benefit from this business idea. No matter what one has studied in school, understanding your true desire is very important. I know what you are thinking, 'there is no capital.' It is no longer a problem. A business analyst and enterprising physician, Norman Vincent Peale once say that "Empty pocket never held anyone back. Only empty heads and empty minds can do that."

When the power of desire supersedes your fear of failure, you will no longer worry about failure because failure is also a state of the mind.

Successful business owners understood their true desires, made the correct goals and then achieved them. And this is what has held most men down and not really lack of capital, no sufficient power, or water. Man has to free his doubts and fears, and believe in himself and his abilities. This is one of the major components needed to achieve life goals. It's in man. No one can make man fail except his mind condition.

Being constantly criticized by friends, family members, and society tends to rob man of his self-worth and self confidence. But man should be in charge of his world. Instead of asking 'why me?' when you meet setback, you can choose to ask 'how come?' Your thoughts can cause you to change your motive and appearance. It can effect or affect your abilities. Take good care of your appearance. When you look better, it changes the way society interacts with you and the way you carry yourself. Ignore any and all destructive criticisms and insults. Your opinion of yourself is the most important opinion of all. Take it one at a time and it will make you feel in charge, and secure in you the ability to make good choices; and you will gain confidence in yourself.

Consider understanding all the instructions given in chapter one on choice making, in building and execution of your decisions. Do not go in contact with things that will make you feel inferior and insecure. Listen to motivational speeches and do not play music that criticises your immediate environment. Through many methods and procedures unknown to man, the subconscious mind begins to shape man upon what he hears, believes and accepts.

Man may not entirely control his subconscious mind but when he makes up his mind to do good things, that is, aiding his subconscious mind with right desire and good plans, he will accomplish them if he uses dynamic willpower to follow through. No matter what the challenges are, if he goes on trying, there is always another road he has not taken, which was created by God for man's desire to find its proper reward. Man need to work step-by-step every day in the direction of his dominant aspiration with unshakeable level of self confidence which will make him virtually unstoppable.

So should man simultaneously work on strengthening his self-discipline and using it to achieve his desire, he will become a better, stronger, and more powerful person. Man should cast out the bonds of helplessness and should begin to know that there is nothing in the world that he cannot do, be or achieve. The evidence of creative efforts will naturally manifest when man sets his desire, and determine to become the kind of person who is capable of achieving the kind of goals that he wants to achieve. He should convince himself at a deep subconscious level that he is absolutely unstoppable.

Four

Achieving Your Desire

Finally, you have found your passion. You're certain you are not imitating other person's life but what God blessed you with. You can confidently describe it without stumbling or guessing. Certainly you will understand what I'm about to say because most of it has continued as long as people lived. There is no suffering for those who live in harmony with the commandments of their minds. They create their lives and they can also recreate them too. If the elements you found in you sincerely meet your personal passion, and you have decided to dedicate yourself and your resources to achieve a successful living in using them. My message to you is very simple. Bear it in mind that there are lots of side attractions, and manifestation of these attractions may increase as you move nearer or closer in achieving your desire. But, it's fun. This is time for you to start seeing yourself as a special person with a true willpower and unique purpose in life. You will soon understand why it's not everyone that can make a living in doing what they love doing.

A man who becomes successful is the man who has the sound of his mind (his inner man) out of lock and key. Believe that achieving your desire can be quite simply. It requires you to take actions that are congruent with your inner man in order to translate your desire into its equivalent in reality. As you already know, there is no desire or dream that is not achievable. "Every mosquito has its own insecticide" - Utowhare Ruth Omokiniovo. You will just have to follow the ***basic principles of success*** to resolve the equation of every setback. Principles which will propel you to achieve a state of equilibrium in your business idea or job performance and then in becoming successful. These Principles are not dark shadows. They have no short-cut. You just have to follow them till a lasting time.

You need to accept, in reality, to be committed, persistent, positive thinking, determined, have faith, be focused, and concentrate your resources to one worthy end. Nature has already made the man on the journey of success in control of materials which reach his subconscious mind. In most instances, there will be friends, family members or even most mentors who will tell you that you will not or simply cannot achieve your dream. They will tell you there is no capital, no electricity, or security. They will not tell you there is a better road just ahead. They will not tell you how to raise capital and most of them can make you feel insecure. They will tell you that you're still young, that you do not have any experience yet. These are the seventy percent of people who once had a dream but have now settled for less. Most people's fate gets worse. They are friends or family members who once studied one professional course in university, college, or polytechnic believing that one day they will become ***doctors, writers, music/movie producers, estate managers, accountants, book publishers, engineers, barristers, singers, footballers, poultry owners, business people*** and so on. But their experiences of life had somehow created fear and insecurity in them and they surrendered their dreams reluctantly. Those passionate dreams are not dead yet. They still live somewhere deep down within their minds. But they no longer believe that they are achievable. Most of them are the ones their friends questioned their ability, doubted their chances, and told them that they themselves once had the same dreams. Those friends told them they need to grow up and be more reasonable and life would just work out very well. Maybe your family members had told you they once had such ambition, but life in Nigeria provided few of those chances and possibilities. They buried fear into your charges, rather than motivating you. Or they had told you that there are no just enough opportunity in the land, that the leaders are irresponsible, that you just have to hang your clothes around where you can reach them, and now you are about to settle for less. They didn't tell you to aim big. They misinterpreted for you that people who aim big are people with rich parents. They didn't tell you that people who stay at home to produce items with local materials aim big. Perfumes, school chalks, soaps, deodorants, air fresheners, water gums, writing, singing, dancing, and so on are achievable within a little space of arena. They haven't told you.

That was how, gradually, their beliefs about life were changed and they came to believe that it would not be possible to reach the heights they had once dreamed of, and so they made their choices to settle for less. Now, most of them are in small business, some are trading, while some are under paid. They are now mediocrities who know the perfect roads but can't drive the car. It's all right. Today, they struggle to pay school fees. They can't meet with hospital bills which have now made them to employ the idea of self medication. They pay up their house rents in two or three folds, or in little instalments. They just can't understand life. They are now like auto-mechanics who do not own a car. They are wrong. I tell you, it's every day focus and if you can make it through the night, there is a brighter day. After all these negative circumstances and challenges, only a few of these passionate **_writers, singer, plumbers, engineers, graphic designers, paint producers, book publishers, doctors, poultry farmers,_**

soap producers, accountants in-the-making are able to stay focused to their dominant aspirations. This explains reasons why a job opportunity is an affair of the head while entrepreneurship is that of the mind.

After you have accepted, as a reality, the existence of willpower, do not let your dreams be strangled out of you owing to environmental traits. Put in your mind that in case you let your dream be strangled out and you once again regain bearing, you really need to be aware that you are still not immune to these environmental challenges. These challenges are what make life meaningful. They were here twenty years ago and will be here twenty years to come. The river flows into the sea yet the sea is not yet full. It's as simple as that. They are the bitter salt that makes a sweeter food.

There will still be most friends and family members who are ready to explain to you how what you are doing now or what you are about doing will not survive. Most of these people are the thirty-seven percent of people who will become jealous when you get to the top. Opportunity in the land is unlimited. It is also a matter of who you keep around you and what you nurse in your mind. If you remain idle and fail to define your desire, your mind will feed upon the materials which reach it as a result of your negligence. Man already experiences, as a result of purified mind, a wider chance. Napoleon Hill understood this statement when he says "Both poverty and riches are the off-spring of thought." Do not think you are to continue waiting for employment opportunity if it did not come so fast. Every man has more options available to him than he realizes. Throughout the walks of life, there are **principles** which will guide you get across the bridge **after schooling** and foster a complete chances of living success despite all circumstances and environments instead. You should understand that your nation is not against you, family members, friends, including Nigerian government wish you a complete living success.

THE BASIC PRINCIPLES OF SUCCESS
(1) Positive Thinking

If actually what every man is experiencing is called "life" then there are chances that every man is suffering to stay alive. But positive thinkers are healthier and less stressed. They have greater overall well-being. Chances are good that people who make enough fortune and wealth in sincerity, in life, are positive thinkers. Even if positive thinking does not come naturally to you, there are plenty of great reasons to start cultivating affirmative thoughts and minimizing negative self-talk. We are all much more than we would've become because of the negative things that we've experienced along the journey of life. Think about the challenges you're having now and try to adjust your feelings and see the good in them. I am not unaware that many people have experienced betrayal, cheating, lies and so on. The truth is that you cannot allow your journey to living success to get corrupted. There is still time, and you need to **keep moving**. If you're currently unemployed, just know that you're being given the chance to organize your life and bring out the best you can.

How do you suppose society feels about you if you're unemployed; for that reason, becoming unsuccessful? Hmm, do not think you will have to react to environmental traits or accept the conditions it foists on you. Sometimes you will have to analyze it and take actions to change it. When faced with stressful situations, being optimistic rather than pessimistic thinking helps you cope more effectively. Think of what you want to achieve in few years ahead and know it's achievable, and then keep moving towards achieving it. Most people have accepted defeat because they feel they can't achieve their aims, it's wrong. I have mentioned that your mind can have a powerful effect on your body, and only positive thinking can generate immunity which is one area where your thoughts and attitudes can have, particularly, a powerful influence on you.

Of all understanding, it is important to note that positive thinking is all about positive approach to ugly situations and general challenges of life. It is trying to make the most of bad situation with certain believe that you are more powerful than the situation. As man is preparing to influence and control himself and listen to his 'inner audience', it is essential that he also understand that bad things will unavoidably happen. Sometimes you will be disappointed or hurt by the actions of friends, family members or society where you find yourself. This does not mean that the world is clamping down against you and your ambition, or that all people will let you down. There are still people who may not want to discourage you, they are ready to walk with you hand in hand till a lasting time. Always remember this.

Positive thinking often starts with self-talk. It is a dependable way to generate strength and willpower to look at situation realistically and search for ways that you can improve it.

(2) Commitment

Life is like an exercise book in which whatever you write in it is what you will see and accept. Meanwhile, the more you write, the more you increase the word-count of your note. That exercise book is your mind which bears you to take control of your potential willpower to dedicate a reasonable amount of time and energy towards achieving your desire. Commitment and good performance are essential elements of a successful business organization no matter the health of the economy, or challenges in one's immediate environment. Believe in your endeavour more than anybody else. I think I overcame every single one of my personal shortcomings by the borne passion I brought to my work. I don't know if you're born with this kind of passion, or if you can learn it. But I do know you need it. If you love your work, you'll be out there every day trying to do the best you can in any way possible, and sooner than you may realize your success will spread faster like a fever. One of the laws of Isaac Newton states that, "To every action, there is an equal and opposite reaction". This law is very true and applicable to the everyday-changing business community. Do not accept negative opinions, talks or influences of the critics who surround you to overpower you. Do not speak or think negatively, be **committed**. What you do now will determine who you will become or where you will be in time to come. Everybody can get at the top but not everybody will get there. If you want to get there, and on time, you're required to stake a reasonable amount of time, money, and other resources to get there; and you're also required to leave no possible means of returning to stage one when you meet setback.

Most people stay connected to the internet, on social networks throughout the entire day. Verily I tell you, this is a true distraction and lack of pure commitment if your business is not done on internet. No matter how you may look at it, at the end, you will reason that this is actually an activity you should put out of your task-list.

(3) Persistence

Any employable graduate or undergraduate can come up with up with a business idea, but not every one of them has the ability to achieve success in his business idea. For you to achieve ultimate success, you have to do something, and keep doing it because it does not end there. Riches and wealth will only come to you when there is constant persistence. It is this quality that allows you to employ your back-up plan over and over again when you meet setback. **Persistence** is an element which when mixed with unshakeable momentum of **self-confidence** will explain the level of one's **willpower**. Learn to identify distractions and ignore them when they come because surely they will unavoidably surface on your journey to living success. And they often come from within.

Consider that this journey of success is like a journey of war where casualties are unavoidable. A man who embarks on the journey of successful living **after schooling** should understand that a soldier neither flees a war, nor returns without his medal and boot. That same way, consider that success is a must because failure is nothing but a reproach. When difficulties or maybe failure approach you at one stage, just know that before success comes to a man who begins a journey of success, he's sure and ready to meet with temporary defeat; he does not truly fail. But each time he meets failure at one stage, he has succeeded in finding a way that it does not work and will apply to the way it does work and continue trying. Every thing else will become easier once you try again. Because through examining your experiences of failure, you can gain true knowledge that will propel you to success.

(4) Faith

In the beginning, when the going may seem difficult and slow, it is only those who have good magnitude of **faith** that will enjoy a lasting insurance against failure even with a number of setbacks. The first commandment of faith states that "**You cannot know everything when you first set out on a business adventure. You only need to have *faith* that what you're doing or about to do will fit into the big scheme of things.**" When you have faith, you will not be bothered by setback. It's only later, along the way when you encounter a certain level of success that you will take your time and recheck to see the impact of your work. If you have faith in what you're doing, you won't be disappointed should you meet failure at first; and your work will eventually come to fruition if you press on. Every failure comes with it the seed of an equivalent success; and equivalent solution to every problem is always available.

Faith is an affair of the mind. It is an inside job. Man, as a spiritual being, must believe and have ***faith***. And he must not limit the result of his request by the thoughts of his own mind. He must allow his faith to decide the best outcome of his belief. Having faith means you have decided to take the calculated risk associated with achieving your goal. It means that you have to stand to your feet if you fall and start all over again because you know that you may meet setback, and it's all right to meet them and also all right to continuously take actions and move forward, because where you fall is not your destination. ***Faith*** rather helps you to take your back-up plan and keep moving, having hope that you will get there in course of time. Just a little more faith in yourself is all your need.

This element, faith, is the hidden justification of life and successful living, not being bored with trials and tribulations. It is the only dependable element whose particles are designed to finally change failure into victory in the course of little time.

I know of a confession by a lady who was travelling from the city of Onitsha to the city of Enugu, in Enugu State. She boarded on a public transportation mini-bus and said her prayers when their journey begun. As the mini-bus of nine passengers took on Enugu-Onitsha express way, they were all delighted and were enjoying their journey until when the bus driver was approached from opposite, a long trailer truck, which was being overtaken by another mini-bus. The driver was able to avert the ghastly accident but, yet, landed into a swap-pit. There was lots of commotion. People rushed to help the dying passengers who were shouting and crying inside the capsized bus. The good news was that none of the boarded passengers died. They were all seriously wounded, yet they lived on. A man in pains of broken legs shouted from his position, "oh, my leg! I'm dying! This is so painful."

When the lady was brought out, she had a dislocation and fracture at her ankle, then broken head too. She shouted, "oh God! Please, I'm in pains! Every other passenger was bleeding from broken heads and so on. And they were all crying in regret. By then, the Road Safety officers had made emergency call for ambulance and the accident victims were being rushed to hospital in Awka, in Anambra State one after the other. The lady was then in greater pains as she chanted and continued chanting, "*I shall not die!*"

When it was time to carry the man with broken legs into the ambulance, he said "I'm tired of all these pains; I can't stand it any more." And as the officers carried him onto a stretcher, he gave up the ghost. Few hours after they were taken to hospital, two of the passengers died. The lady continued her confession "***I shall not die!***" each time she cried in pains and agonies. They were all given medications, but at night, just before dawn, two of the remaining passengers died. The next day, it was remaining only the driver and three of the passengers which included the lady as they were responsive to treatments.

This was power of spoken word mixed with pure faith, which travelled down inside the lady's subconscious mind to build hope of life, and made it manifested for her to live on after all, for she never died inside at first. Through the rightly or wrongly application of spirit behind spoken word, man continues to make law for himself. If there be common understanding, **faith** is the only dependable way of building internal energy and eternal strength to proceed on the external adventure in all walks of life. It is stronger than all food supplements. Only faith can build astonishing hope of seeing a brighter tomorrow.

(5) Focus

Focus is a revolutionary product that can be altered when implementing business intelligence. It is the ability to give all your resources- attention, time, money and energy to achieve a particular desire by gently listening to your mind. Everybody is built differently. It's all about what you feel inside and what you think. The best way to exercise enough of your focus is by finding the way it works for you. Friends and family members may encourage you to employ any strategy to achieve your desire. It's all right. Truly, there is nothing wrong with giving your friends or family members a maximum hearing. But what works for you may not work for them as well. The way you think and see things may not be the way they think and see things.

Only you understand your inner man very well. When people try to make you feel guilt over the time you're devoting to achieve your desire, please persist and remain focused. Your desire is important to you. Those who exercise their focus promptly and definitely know what they want, and generally reach their goals at the end.

Here is a simple reality: if you can't think effectively, you can't focus. And if you can't focus, you definitely can't produce the quality of work necessary to achieve your desired goal and become successful. From this perspective, it's not difficult to see why focus is such an essential tool for business success and successful living.

Man, having conceived a dream, can ensure that he has an ideal focus at achieving success in his business adventure by simply de-cluttering his mind. One thing I'm sure you would agree with me about is that a cluttered mind can't focus, as well as a troubled mind. If your mind is filled with stuff such as all of the things you need to resolve, you won't be able to focus well. Man is tasked by law of success to go through his daily tasks and prioritise them. If you're like most business people, there are items on your calendar that you can either put off to another day, delegate, or not do at all. Clear your mind of anything that doesn't relate to the message coming from your mind, which is in harmony with your way of achieving success. The less clutter you have in your mind, the better you will be able to focus. Through focus upon desire, man's mind emerges the element which becomes a creative faith that can turn the hand wheel of attraction to receptive softness.

If you are an employee seeking an improved job performance, create a focused workspace. It's also not uncommon for workers to have cluttered working environment that include greatest obstacle to being focused in this digital age. Gadgets such as computers, televisions, tablets, hand-phones, and the pings, vibrations and other notifications signalling to you that a mail, text message or social media update has arrived. This is only but a constant source of distraction. They are the elements which break up the straight line of efforts you're emitting on you goal. They always lead to delay to success, and most times, failure.

(6) Determination

Some people may try to influence your strength when they consider their own ability, thinking that you have the same ability as they do, it's all right. They may question your strategy and doubt the possibility of attaining your very goal, **keep moving**. A determined mind is not too far from a focused mind and cannot listen to a weak man. Man must, by his own natural efforts, develop the strength required by his spirit which is necessary to keep moving during and after ugly situations. He who knows this is ready to become something higher and stronger by mere harmonising of his mental power.

In Nigeria, in 1930s, in Ab?okuta of Ogun State, at that time of British dominion, there was a **creative writer** who grew up in an atmosphere of religious syncretism, with influences from both cultures. He took an active role in Nigeria's political history and its struggle for independence from Great Britain. In 1967, during the Nigerian Civil War, he was arrested by the federal government of General Yakubu Gowon and put in solitary confinement for two years. If one talked about people with persistent DETERMINATION, one could talk about the man who seized the Western Nigeria Broadcasting Service Studio and broadcast a demand for the cancellation of the Western Nigeria Regional Elections in 1965. Prof. Wole

Soyinka was a man who had strong DETERMINATION to criticise many Nigerian military dictators by his own natural effort, strength and willpower, especially late General Sanni Abacha, as well as other political tyrannies, including Mugabe regime in Zimbabwe. I'm not trying to criticise any political scheme, neither do I try to cover up any critics or destroy any political efficacy. I'm only here to express the opinion that I have discovered the secrets to identify and conquer fear and failure before they arrive. The secrets are in PERSISTENT - DETERMINATION.

When you travel on your road to living success, break all the bridges that carry you over, and leave no possible means of returning back to stage one. Stake a reasonable amount of willpower to get what you desire, and leave only a back-up plan ready. Fear and failure are affairs of the mind. You should remove them as options. You and your back-up plan simply means and expresses that you're prepared for any eventuality; and should failure occur, with your back-up plan, you're unstoppable until you attain your desire.

(7) Love

Man should consider the power of **love** as a top principle of living success. It is also a known fact that **love** is an affair of the mind which will help man to use his auto-suggestion in understanding his desire and in deciding how every other thing may work for him. If man fills his mind with hatred, contempt, doubts, and does not have regard for things he do, or society, country, or people who may be interested in his end products, it is certain that his success will be limited only to those who he has regard for. Man must not allow his creative protest to degenerate into physical anger, contempt, violence, or hatred. However, I fully realize that no man can truly desire what he does not love and passionate about. Therefore everyone should extend his love and passion and engage in transaction which does benefit all whom it may affect.

I know I will succeed most by attracting to myself the force I wish to use and the cooperation of other people when there is enough **love**. Therefore I will induce others to love me. Because of my love for them, I will eliminate all acts of cheat, selfishness, envy or jealousy; because I understand the language of my inner audience. I know that a negative attitude towards others can never bring me success and happiness. I will cause them to love and believe in me, because I love and believe in them. I'm proud to be a Nigerian and I love my nation. I also understand that positive and negative emotions can occupy the mind at the same time, so I consciously adopt to express that **love** is all we need. So, "**let love lead.**" T. B. Joshua.

Love is the enduring substance of every successful man's virtues. He who loses **dream** loses much, but he who loses **desire** loses much more, and yet, he who loses **love** loses all.

(8) *Prayer*

Prayer happens in the mind only. Seldom does man understand that all stimulation to attain success grows access from the spiritual realm. This access may lead to temporal or long lasting success when the laws of prosperity are not violated. These laws are made or unmade in the spiritual realm through **prayer** and passionate belief only. Man is advised to consider prayer in everything he do. There is no amount of prayer that goes void of correspondence. Through sincere praying, man begins to move things around. Praying is like using a product manual of a machine of which without the product manual of any machine one may find it difficult to use the machine's systematic applications.

From these brief references on the subject, it may be mentally understand that God who is the producer of your soul needs to be consulted in every area of your of life through prayer. Every man has his own mind just like every machine has its own application system. And God has made man as a machine to be used in producing other machines. This simply means that God created man and made him a creator on earth. The widespread ignorance on the subject of prayer is due to a known fact that the subject is surrounded with mystery and silence, and this mystery and silence has an effect on the minds of the youths. Every intelligent person knows that man is a carrier of God's image which simply simplifies every man as a man of God until he violates the commandments of Spiritual Law. Man of all professions, talents and careers has calling from God. It all depends on your **desire** which you have generated within your mind through your own thoughts and choices.

Through prayer, man will understand and define his true desire, which when properly understood, the reason for existence on earth will be achieved.

In life, on the journey of successful living, man is a spiritual being sorting upon human experience. He has a soul which all the movement of his body obeys. A person who is on the journey of successful living, as a spiritual being, should understand that his mind is the carrier of all his true potentials (his natural weapons) which is the bearer of his thoughts. It is only prayer and sincere belief that will propel your desire to fruition. Which when well defined, you will see yourself unlocking all other areas of your life.

God is God everywhere, in every religion. He is in Judaism, in Islam, and in Christianity. He's in the mind of every true believer who obeys the commandments of Spiritual Laws despite your religion. He only comes to man who knows how to reach Him in prayer. He has no specific name, what man calls him is what He becomes. There is no bad religion under Almighty God. There are only bad people in different religions piloting the affairs of man, hence changing their directions and beliefs which is God. Saint Paul understood this when he wrote his first letter to Corinthians to deal with problems of Christian life and faith that had arisen in the church. If you're an intelligent person you will observe that religions have also failed to resort on their main mission owing to factions, while the basic role of church or mosque is not to teach man to resort to a particular denomination or religion. In one same way, all of us under Almighty God, whether Jews or Gentiles, Christians or Muslims were made spiritual beings in one body of God by the same Spirit, and we have all been given the one Spirit to drink. A true system of religion is not about the crowd, it's about the faith. There will not be religion if it were only the Christians, or the Muslims, or Jews, or Gentiles. As it is, there are many religions but only one Almighty God. Man is not to make up the congregation, he is a part of moving and functioning miracle called 'the Church' or 'the Mosque'. It is, therefore, the duty of religion to teach man how to prosper and attain a living success while on earth.

All religions understand that the science of prayer is more than a mere theory. In realization of the power of prayer, Islam also proceeded. Muslims under Almighty God are not terrorists. Christians say, "I follow Jesus Christ", while Muslims say, "I follow Prophet Muhammad", but God cannot be divided into groups. I observed that true Christians and true Muslims used to (and they still do) live together, side by side in Nigeria and in many other nations. Islam is an empire of rigid faith. "When Prophet Muhammad brought the first stanzas of Holy Koran when he returned from mountain where he said Arch-Angel Gabriel appeared to him and revealed that the Koran was the word of God, and that he, Muhammad, was to be a messenger of God, Arch-Angel Gabriel told him one night during Ramadan. He was ordered to recite in prayer:

'Recite in the name of thy **Lord** (God), who created,
'Created **man** from a clot;
'Recite in the name of thy **Lord** (God),
'Who taught by the pen,
'Taught **man** what he knew not.

Prophet Muhammad was not against other religions for he intended not to build a different religion for a different God. His return from Mecca marked the beginning of a new polity. For the first time in Arabia, members of a community were bound together not by the traditional ties of clan and tribe, but by their shared belief in the one true Almighty God. Later, some of the believers, looking back on this event and recognized its seminal importance by designating it as the first year of their new era.

Prophet Muhammad made repeated attempts to attract the Jews and other religions to his course. He directed all believers in a single faith to worship like the Jews in the direction of Jerusalem. Ultimately, these attempts failed, and henceforth, Muslims prayed in the direction of the Kaaba in Mecca, Muhammad's native town; which had long been a centre of paganism. Then, it thereby became the centre of the true religion, the focal point of the believers' daily prayer, and eventually the object of their annual pilgrimage."

However, the Koran still revealed that all man (the Christians, the Muslims, the Jews, the Gentiles, and so on) are equal before Almighty God; that the world should be a democratic republic. This simply expresses that all religions under Almighty God share one particular principle which is "***Equity in Fraternity***." This is a sincere expression of faith and belief to the understanding of man's willpower in life. There is God of love everywhere in different religions; and until you understand the dependable source through which you can reach Him, you cannot understand what ***prayer*** is. When man hears something, or sees something, man is under the law of nature to first examine it in the light of God through prayer. So, do not be a part to division among men. Be completely united, with only one thought and one purpose; which is to be a servant of God and obey the commandments of ***Spiritual Law***.

I imagine some readers will question there is a shortcut to successful living without the afore-mentioned principles. Yes, you're right. But one thing I'm certain about is that the fact that you are reading this book is an indication that you honestly seek knowledge of all kind which this book has provided. And having read to this page is not by chance. You are a subject matter already. There is a greater chance that you may grow higher where employment, business productivity, financial success, and living success are the issues. But you will only grow by assuming an attitude of genuine humility and sincere love. There is no shortcut to living success or acquiring wealth should you choose to employ some of the principles and reject, neglect, or simply refuse to use others you will remain stagnant in life and lagging in business, or in your job performance. To get satisfactory results, you must employ this ***Basic Principles of Success*** in good spirit and in pure faith in the area of your dominant aspirations. I have written to you, not with the knowledge of human wisdom, but I'm here with the message of spiritual wisdom, to make you understand the power of natural law given to man by God and obey it. All the principles of success, of any kind, including prayer is an affair of the mind which makes success a business that any sincere person(s) with a positive mental attitude can attain. These principles are very essential for success in all walks of life. They are laws through which man may control his economic destiny. They lead to power, financial success, wealth and riches, greatness, worldly recognition, happiness and so on. There is magnificent reward for all those who employ the principles outlined herein. This statement is not made to inspire your heart, it is made based upon the knowledge gained of successful men and women whom I had devoted a very long time to classify their principles.

If you want evidence that you can become successful in any venture, consider this book like a lamp in a bedroom. The most expensively furnished bedroom will be in darkness at night without a lamp. This simplifies how a certified graduate without the basic knowledge of principles of living success is. It is like connecting an expensive television or radio set to a wall socket without electricity. No matter how high you turn on the volume-button on the television set, there will be no sound. Certificate may offer job opportunity, but it does not guarantee successful living. It is only the utilization of the principles of successful living when employed can make employee become an employer of labour and unemployed youth become a business owner.

A man with these basic principles is **Majority**. It can begin in the form of mindset. Thought is like the light of life to man. When you put on a small light, your view is within, but when you put on a big light, your view is widened. Not to have good thought is like putting off all the elements of light in the darkest bedroom. The amount of desire is limited only by the person in whose mind the desire is being generated. Always remember this when you're ready to bargain with life; ***there is gold everywhere***. In the light of this truth, also remember it is not sufficient to say "God should grant my desire." Man does not get what he wishes or prays for if his thoughts and actions are not in harmony with the ***laws*** of achieving what he seek. This is the simplest essential fact of the principles I declare to you, to rise up and attain your living success.

However, circumstances of man can be so complicated. Individual's happiness varies vastly upon condition of belief and understanding, of the fate of unemployment. It is importantly redemptive for educational institutions to teach potential graduates and undergraduates how to venture into business ideas or establish on what they have learned. And also how to succeed in those business ideas they venture into. Get them to start building a solid desire and unshakeable level of self confidence towards achieving successful living from, and in those lucrative ideas emerging from courses which they have studied in the institutions. "The function of education is to teach one to think intensively and to think critically. Intelligence plus character that is the goal of true education." Martin Luther.

For many reasons, it is properly fit to influence the future of students a hundred years before they're graduated. It seemed quite significant to me when I made the discovery that every unemployed graduate whom I had the privilege of interviewing was eventually doing something to survive and gain financial freedom. The circumstances which most of these graduates find themselves revealed to them their true self and intelligence. They happen to be the products of formal education only.

Learning does not just happen in a classroom or from a book alone. Acquiring the knowledge of financial intelligence does not take place in school at all. This is not the same knowledge acquired in business schools or faculty of management sciences. There is depth of knowledge which will inject some practical fun into learning about money and investment. The result of simple application of this knowledge has increased curiosity and the desire to practice more. Upon considering your financial statement, this knowledge will help you to build your assets and wealth. It is a formula of financial budgeting from a carefully made financial analysis to help design a financial guideline which will help people learn about money, how it works and how to accumulate riches from a monthly cash flow. In application of this systematic formula, you are able to track all your invisible expenditures and improve your savings. Accept there is noticeable evidence that you will begin to do the best of your financial life before the age ahead. Most employees who have not done the best of their financial life have not got, and have not applied this systematic formula. Do not doubt me about this because there is plenty of evidence to prove it. People who become financially independent and have acquired blessed wealth are generally the people who are often creative and can track their expenses after they have taken all calculated risks to make income. There are lots of people who are gainfully employed, though their salaries and benefits are not meagre, yet they do not get ahead financially. This world is filled with people like that; a group of motley collections of smart, talented, educated, gifted, and most of them are simply employed. We meet them every day. They are part of the reasons why school leavers float on air owing to insufficient job opportunity because these talented and smart people have not become successful to liquidate from their employers for new employees to move in. These talented, smart, gifted, or educated employees and business people need to study the diagram below and notice if they can pick up some distinctions. Again, it has to do with understanding your cash flow, which tells the story. Most people look at their financial statement and balance sheet and then miss the story. These people are all around us in bank industries, factories, production companies, one business or the other. They think that when they graduate and find themselves in one job opportunity, business, career or the other, that money will grow into their banks' accounts. It is with this mental attitude that they deal with their life challenges with all their financial strength without considering the corresponding speed and level of their cash flow. All they need is only one sound idea; to learn and master on this financial skills so as to acquire financial intelligence. I have mentioned before that your liquid fund is your potential power, and financial intelligence is all about the ability to account; knowing '*where to credit* and '*when to credit*, '*where to debit* and '*why you should debit*, with a guiding law of CASH-FLOW. When you master all these four technical skills, your financial strength will be increased with ease.

When it comes to schooling, institutions of higher learning generally have one basic teaching and orientation they give to students. And that is, **work very hard to earn a standard degree or diploma certificate so as to be gainfully employed.** But being gainfully employed does not, and will not guarantee an upgrade in your financial management. Without financial intelligence people are as good as being unemployed, for they are working and labouring for nothing but for money. Only earning money they have no knowledge of how to control, direct, credit, or deposit.

Believe there is an unsolved myth existing within every working class men and women that is responsible for an increase in spending each time there is an increase in income. This myth is the one responsible for lack of money, because people graduate without financial skills and business intelligence. If you adopt the cash-flow guideline shown below, you will soon realize what is missing from the education acquired by every graduate who think that working harder is the only answer. You will understand how a rich man is nothing but a poor man with money. As a proof of lack of this knowledge, we all know most people who become dependent again when they are no longer able to work.

Consider utilizing this formula obtained from a strategic financial analysis of how monthly cash flow should be utilized:

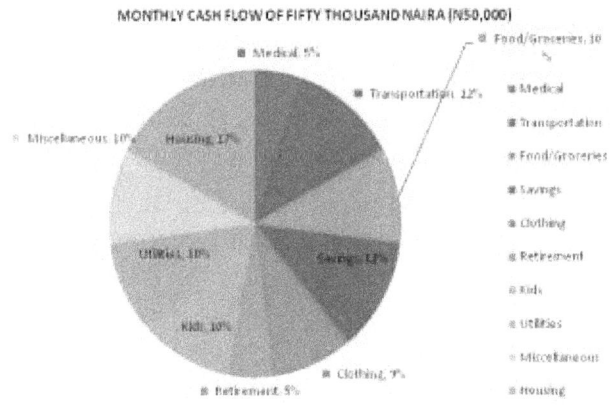

"Where should my monthly income be going to? **One sound advice is what you need.** When it really comes down to that question, the answer is different for everyone. You may be in a hurry to pay off debt, so you're not willing to spend more on clothing in the meantime. Or you may live in a city where house rent is prohibitively expensive, so you have to allocate more of your income to housing.

So, what sound guideline does a person need? While I can't give you a quick and fast rule for where and how to spend your money, but, after an accurate financial analysis and research, I have come with a general benchmark to consider if you're not under-paid or you're just starting to set up a financial budget as a first time employee.

Whether you're a parent with kids, a recent graduate working your first job or undergraduate building a career around your beloved talents or hobbies, this guideline can help you not only to figure out how much you may want to allocate to each area of your life every month. But it can also help you to determine the order in which your money can be allocated. It can walk you from middle class to upper class if you're disciplined enough.

Consider putting down your budget percentage according to your income and responsibilities. What matters is one's respect to the **law** of operating the **guideline**. It will help you build a secured financial foundation.

Example: A youth who is just boarding on the journey of financial success, who has a fixed monthly income, can operate with the above percentages outlined in the analysis, in the chart. This does not express that if you do not have a fixed monthly income you should not operate with the above percentage on each areas of expenditure, of course you can. The only difference is that your monthly budget breakdown will not vary every month. I have this explanation to express, using the above chart of monthly cash flow of fifty thousand naira (N50, 000), you will resolve these:

MONTHLY CASH FLOW (N50, 000.00)				
Expenditure	Percentage %	Value	Month	One Year (x12)
Utilities	10%	$\frac{10 \times 50,000}{100} =$	N5, 000	N60, 000
Housing	17%	$\frac{17 \times 50,000}{100} =$	N8, 500	N102, 000
Food/Groceries	10%	$\frac{10 \times 50,000}{100} =$	N5, 000	N60, 000
Medical Care	5%	$\frac{5 \times 50,000}{100} =$	N2, 500	N30, 000
Transportation	12%	$\frac{12 \times 50,000}{100} =$	N6, 000	N72, 000
Miscellaneous	10%	$\frac{10 \times 50,000}{100} =$	N5, 000	N60, 000
Savings	12%	$\frac{12 \times 50,000}{100} =$	N6, 000	N72, 000
Retirement	5%	$\frac{5 \times 50,000}{100} =$	N2, 500	N30, 000
Kids	10%	$\frac{10 \times 50,000}{100} =$	N5, 000	N60, 000
Clothing	9%	$\frac{9 \times 50,000}{100} =$	N4, 500	N54, 000
Total =	100%	*******	N50, 000	N 600, 000

This rule recommends that you allocate 50% of your budget for essentials (housing, transportation, medical care, utilities and groceries), 20% towards financial priorities (retirement contributions, savings, and debt payments), and the remaining 30% for lifestyle expenses (clothing, fun, etc). If you're a parent, there are responsibilities to consider while advancing through the cash flow guideline. Get a ledger notebook and draw your own monthly budget in harmony with your family weight. The outlined percentages in the chart above may not be the best for you to adopt. Understand that it is not set in stone either, because everyone has different priorities. Most people have gone past the time necessary to implement this financial guideline, and those are the forty percent of people who altered the principles of ***time*** and ***living success***. But read and understand just as needed, and be disciplined enough to stick with what you decide upon.

The only thing to do with good advice is to pass it on. It is never of any use to hold it back. If you take this knowledge, you will have a great financial management and upgrade. The information shown above is for illustrative purposes only and it's not intended as investment advice. Until you master this financial guideline, so you may be able to track your spending and visualize your budget.

Schooling is an admirable thing, but it is better to remember from time to time that it is not every thing that is worth knowing can be taught in institution of higher learning. Yet, there is no limit to the level of education man can acquire. This table expresses the great secret of managing funds, after having been put to practical test by number of successful paid workers, people in business, and entrepreneurs, it is now made available to reach all people who do not have enough time to workout how wealthy people accumulate riches.

Time shall come when no one will approach the universal mind of the youths in a state of fear and discouragement owing to insufficient job opportunity and financial downturn. A great number of employable graduates have experienced not getting what they should get, which is financial freedom and living success. Such is not a good life. They cannot have it their own way all the time. They have to adapt to the people around them and to society where they live in, it's all right. This is also the part of financial skills which I seek should be taught and expressed in all institutions of higher learning worldwide. The rightful application of this formula worth more than a thousand claps. Because everyone who knows *Learn Vest Planning Services* knows it's an honest statement. It does not have room for, or causes shortage in management of funds.

For most of "want-to-be" entrepreneurs and others who wish to grow their entrepreneurial business into something bigger and better, those who have true passion for business ideas mentioned in the next chapter of this book, every single business idea counts for something bigger. Abraham Lincoln once say, "Give me six hours to chop down a tree and I will spend the first four hours sharpening the axe." I tell you, when everybody is looking for job opportunity, then it is no longer an issue of job opportunity. The system born in the conventional method of job security, pension, and job benefits is dying out. A new conventional method is emerging, an economic system known to few graduates and educators too little in number.

If you believe this prophecy is not near reached, by mere reading of this book, take a close look at your mind and listen to your inner audience, if you have just experienced an inner shift over this prospect, then **magnificent** you have become. All the business ideas mentioned herein are easy and lucrative. Most people will not like to practice new ideas as long as the old ones still exist. Yet, **Keep Moving**.

Five

Consider Your Passion

A Native American grandfather was chatting with his grandson. He said "I feel as if I have two big wolves fighting in my heart. One wolf is the vengeful, violent one and the other wolf is the loving compassionate one." His grandson asked him, "Father, which one of the wolves will win the battle?" and the grandfather replied to him, "The one I feed." Blackhawk. Consider your passion and know which one to feed. Choosing a goal and sticking to it can change everything. If you don't have passion for it you won't take care of it.

As a young man, my father advised and encouraged me to find a safe job ***after schooling***, one that has good salary and beautiful benefits. He took my 'curriculum vitae', including my already made cover letter and called his brothers, my uncles, and his friends to announce my graduation to them. He made copies of my papers and sent to them. I knew what he was doing, this was the one he fed. But on the other hand, I encouraged myself and found a mechanic workshop where I could learn how to run a monthly car servicing like changing of brake pads, changing of engine oil, injector and carburettor servicing, clutch servicing and other services. This was the one I fed. I chose to learn this because I desire to own a mechanic workshop of my own. I love car painting so I would look for a reliable station where I would learn that too. Upon the understanding of my nature, my mother calls me **MACHINE**. I desire, with great passion and sincere love, to run a mechanic workshop. I could look at machine tools all day-long and when problems arise, the problems are not so strong that it would change my passion for machine tools and maintenance. For such people who do not like machine tools and would not like to learn how to use them should not bother about owing a mechanic workshop. I love construction and welding of any kind. If you ask me, I would say it's all about creativity. In the year 2011, during my final year project, in department of mechanical engineering, I was assigned to design and construct a Circular Saw Machine with capacity of 1800rev per min. Eight months after the project presentation, I was contracted to optimize the design of the Circular Saw Machine with capacity of 2000 revolution per minute and a locomotive control panel to effect the depth of cut and angle of cut. Since the former's control panel was fixed, and the foundation design was done in such a way that the workbench could only accommodate sheets of materials not bigger than 609.6mm by 1219.2mm and 6mm depth of cut, and had no vice. So, I redesigned the cutting machine with the specifications. If you have the opportunity to see the machines, you will understand that creativity had worked. I enjoyed my time during the designing and construction of the machines to the heart. It was not an enormous undertaking. It was simply creativity, and I love creativity. I respect the spirit of creativity for it seems to be the only one left in the world of job creation.

If you find passion with car maintenance and would want to practice, always remember that there is achievement in every failure. You can use my strategy which is to start small and keep moving no matter what the matter is. Learn from people who practice daily. You alone will express what you feel. No one will do that for you. Somebody who studied mechanical engineering or other related courses and have passion and desire for being a practising mechanical engineer can start with:
-car air conditioner repair and servicing,

-injector, clutch, carburettor servicing,
-machine design and construction,
-car painting service, and so on.

Success is an affair of the mind should you be thinking it won't bring you a complete living success. This is where your thought will influence your subconscious mind. If you love it and wish to practice it, do it with passion. And remind yourself from time to time that success is a step to step progress; and wealth and riches only come to those who open their minds to the environmental opportunities. I know most people would want to be self employed without seeking a job opportunity if success were guaranteed. But in reality, it was; only if you **keep moving**.

Financial Agency

If you have studied financial studies like accountancy and finance, business administration, insurance, banking and finance, marketing and business, or public administration you can benefit from this business idea. This does not mean that if you are a cooperate person, or you have keen interest in mathematics, or in a career involving finance and business that you should not venture, of course you can venture. Why I'm passionate about this business idea is because I discovered it and can testify for the goodness that comes from doing it. By following the laid down instructions in chapter four of this book, the seat of financial freedom is reserved for you. It requires only a bank account or bank accounts that are internet banking-enabled and a laptop that is internet-enabled too. A liquid capital of (depending on your target) fifty thousand naira can do a new thing.

There are books that deal on addressing the public which you can use to master yourself on how to handle traders and the general public. Consider "Greatest Salesman in the World" by Og Mandino: This short book offers a wealth of advice on being better at sales, public speaking and influencing the general public or "How to Win Friends and Influence People" by Dale Carnegie. But this does not mean you cannot start with friends and family members within your reach who are into buying and selling, including servicing. There is a maximum guarantee that they will introduce you to their neighbours and customers in less than one month if you make use of your dynamic willpower to follow up. Do not forget to secure for yourself an identity card bearing your details as a financial agent.

My analysis from the investigation I carried out on this business idea revealed that one can generate about twenty thousand naira in a week (six working days). A maximum transfer of fund does not exceed N200, 000 in a single transaction, and daily transaction is not more than two million naira (N2, 000,000) only. A testimony which came from my friend Mr. Henry Madukwe who has benefited from this business idea stated that he generated not less than seventy-five thousand naira in a month (twenty-eight working days) after balancing his expenses from transportation, feeding, and other miscellaneous expenses. Actually, I'm not in doubt because he was once a gainfully employed marketing officer with one of the successful bank- Sterling Bank; which gave him a "go" about how to convince people.

His transfer rate goes between one hundred to two hundred naira for each transfer, depending.
- A transfer of N25, 000 or less from his account to the beneficiary account in the same bank attracts N100 to him; if it goes to a different bank, it attracts N200 into account. (N100 is the charge fee of transfers going to other

banks)

- A transfer of not less than N25, 000 and not more than N80, 000 from his account to the beneficiary account attracts to him N200 or N300; to other banks attracts N300 or N400 naira only. (N100 is the charge fee of transfers going to other banks.)

- A transfer of not less than N80, 000 or not more than N150, 000 attracts between N400 and N500 only, to any banks. And it goes on like this. (Yet, N100 is the charge fee of transfers going to other banks.)

One funny thing about this business idea is that he makes more money when he transacts small funds between N3, 000 - N20, 000 within his bank. Recently, most of his funds transfer is done at home to the beneficiary account base on phone calls from most of his clients. The business idea has exploded beyond his capacity as he ventured into the exchange lane in the market and added four clients which brought his number of clients beyond his capacity. Any single transaction between the sum of three hundred thousand and five hundred thousand naira is done in three transfers, and it attracts between N700 and N800 respectively.

Do not settle for lesser than you can make for yourself. Upon troubles and pains coming from inner crisis, lack of self worth, and lack of self-confidence you will continue to survive. "To be successful, you must decide exactly what you want to accomplish, and then resolve to pay the price to get it." - Bunker Hunt. I would also recommend paint making for most people who have desire and passion for chemical mixtures.

Paint Production

I sincerely welcome this business idea. I shall be

suggesting solutions in paint making, with emphasis on Emulsion paint. Yet, Textcoat, Nylon or Washable Paint is also worthwhile and profitable. But I would recommend a complete manual on paint making for full knowledge, yet this will guide you. Paint production is simpler than you realize. It requires the love for chemical mixtures and endurance. Once you're able to learn how and when to apply chemical elements, there is a guarantee that you will soon become employer of labour.

Introduction of Chemicals

These are chemicals used in the production of paints

.FUNCTIONS OF THE CHEMICALS

1. Water: Water serves a as solvent in the production process. Just like other diluents such as organic oil, petroleum based-oil or other synthetic liquids. The main purpose is to dissolve the polymer and adjust the viscosity of the paint. It is volatile and does not become part of the paint film. It dries off when applied. It also controls flow and application properties, and in some cases, diluents (solvent) can affect the stability of the paint while in liquid state. Its main function is to carry the non volatile components. It can combine the materials more easily during mixing.

2. Titanium dioxide: Also known as titanium (IV) oxide or titanium. It is a type of pigment; white-solid in appearance and odourless, and it is insoluble in water and non-inflammable. During usage, the melting point is 1843 °C while it boils at 2972 °C. When used as a pigment, it is called pigment-white 6 (PW6). It is mainly sourced from limonite ore. This is the most widespread form of titanium dioxide-bearing ore around the country. You can always get it where they are selling paint chemicals, or rather industrial chemicals. It performs the function of making sure that your paint is shiny and not dull.

3. Calcium Carbonate: This chemical also falls under the category of natural pigment. It is a compound chemical with molecular formula $CaCO_3$. It is also in fine-white powdery form, chalky taste and odourless. It is also called limestone or calcite, but different from Calcium Bicarbonate. It is commonly used medicinally as a calcium supplement or as an antacid, but excessive consumption can be hazardous.

4. Colourants: This element is incorporated in the paint to contribute colour. It is an important element during production process. It involves the ability of mixing some elements to get a desired colour. It is not difficult if you have initiative and artistic eye. Yellow, blue, red are all primary colours (primary colours- they can be used in production of other colours) All other colours are secondary colours which is gotten from a proportional combination of one or two of primary colours.

In production of white paint, you do not have to mix colours to get white paint. Pure white paints are resulted as evidence of $CaCo_3$. In fact, once you add your calcium carbonate in water you get white paint.

I will explain how to mix the paints to get a particular desired result. But for now just know that colours can be found in paste or oxide. When I say colours are in paste I mean that they are in condensed liquid form (like your pomade), when they are in oxide it means they are in dust form (powder-like). Such colour like cream has both oxide and paste. Red and black are mostly in oxide, green and blue are in paste. For those who might be wondering which one to use between the yellow oxide and yellow paste, I suggest if you want a complete yellow colour you should use paste; for light-yellow (30-40 yellow colour paint) use oxide.

CAUTION: Colours are diluted very well with a little water before you apply it to your paint. For example if you have a red oxide, pour little water in a different container and mix thoroughly. If not, there will be dots stains on the painted walls.

5. Binders: This is the film form. The binder imparts adhesion and strongly influences properties such as gloss, durability, flexibility and toughness. These elements called binders include synthetic or natural resins such as alkyds, acrylics, vinyl-acrylics (P.V.A), vinyl acetate/ethylene (VAE), polyurethanes polyesters, melamine resins, epoxy, or oils.

Binders can be categorized according to the mechanisms for drying or curing. Although drying may refer to evaporation of the solvent or thinner. It usually refers to oxidative cross-linking of the binders, and is indistinguishable from curing. Some paints form by solvent evaporation only, but most rely on cross-linking processes

. **6. Additives**: Paints can be made in variety of miscellaneous additives, which are usually added in small amounts, yet provide a significant effect on the product. Some example include additives to modify surface tension, improve flow properties, improve the finished appearance, increase wet edge, improve pigment stability, impart antifreeze properties, control foaming, control skinning, etc. Other types of additives include catalysts, thickeners, stabilizers, emulsifiers, texturizers, adhesion promoters, UV stabilizers, flatteners (de-glossing agents), and biocides to fight bacterial growth.

7. Fillers: These are special type of pigments that serve to thicken the film too. It supports its structure and increase the volume of the paint. Fillers are usually cheap and inert materials such as diatomaceous earth, talc, lime, barites, clay, marble dust, etc.

Steps to making Emulsion Paints

Paint production is a physical process which can involve mixing, grinding, weighing, tinting, thinning and packaging; so there is no much chemical reactions involve that you cannot stand. This production process may be carried out in a large mixing drum or tank depending on your target. It involves the following process-

*Dissolution of solid materials.

*Mixing of different elements in right proportion or liquids with solid materials.

*Further mixing of materials may be to fulfil certain specifications with regard to viscosity, colour, and so on.

*Most production process may include sieving and filtering of base materials, intermediate end product.

These dispersions are prepared by emulsion polymerization. Such paints cure by a process called coalescence where at first, the water, and then the trace, or coalescing, solvent, evaporate and draw together and soften the binder particles and fused them together into irreversibly bound networked structures, so that the paint cannot re-dissolve in the solvent/water that originally carried it.

This paint type known as emulsion in Nigeria, Ghana, Madagascar, United Kingdom, etc, is also called Latex in USA and few other countries. It is a water-borne dispersion of sub-micrometer polymer particles. These terms in their respective countries cover all paints that use synthetic polymers such as acrylic, vinyl acrylic (PVA), styrene acrylic, etc as binders. You need to be aware that there are other types of paint as well. For example, satin, oil, etc. But, I shall be treating emulsion/latex.

? Step 1

Mix Calcium Carbonate or any other pigment such as clays, mica, calcite clays, blanc fixe, precipitated calcium carbonate, silica, or talc in a bucket of water. When you add calcium to water, the water level will increase.

NOTE: If you are producing white paint, you will mix titanium (IV) oxide or pigment white-6 in water before adding calcium.

? Step 2

Now, after you have mixed it very well, you may put your colour. It is assumed that by now you must have diluted the colours as required with water if they are oxide. Add colours in small rations and keep stirring the compound until you get your desired result. You can always add more colours if you like. Suppose you added more yellow than you needed to, you can correct it by adding more calcium (but not after this stage) Bear it in mind that the colour may be deeper when wet and lighter when the paint is dried. It is advised you get manual book on mixing colours.

? Step 3

Mix your binder to the compound. I suggest vinyl-acrylics. Vinyl-acrylic is white and powdery so you need to dilute it in a half tin of water before using it and turn it very well. Vinyl-acrylic is used as adhesives for porous materials. Only this element can also be used as coating to protect cheese from fungi and humidity, this is also why it is mixed to the compound. Stir very well at any addition of a new chemical.

? Final Step

When you have completed the above steps, make sure that

you mix the above chemicals very well. As you are stirring it, you may be a little fidgeted that you have wasted your resources. You don't need to be afraid. Just add additive to the mixture and continue stirring. Add it in small quantity until you get the thickness you desire. However, if you add excess you may spoil your mixture. Now that your paint is ready, just take your scraper, brush and roller and make a little testing.

Warning: Please the chemicals must be applied with the laid down procedures; though I am free to state here that these procedures are worthy of your own analysis. But if you apply them systematically as instructed, there won't be any complications.

What gives you wealth and success is not what you do to earn a living but how you do it to achieve your goal. Success will come if you continue to do things right. If you can secure for yourself an incubator, and wish to run birds production, you can start for yourself a lucrative business of hatching birds' eggs such as chickens.

Birds Production (Hatching Eggs)

This production is good once you have love and passion for birds. It is in harmony with poultry farming as well. Secure an incubator and an area where it can stay, then start at once. Supply your eggs (fertilized eggs) to your incubator every seven days. This means you will run the production process every seven days after twenty-one days of the first supply into the incubator.

Eggs should hatch in 21days, though some may hatch a day or two days earlier and some a day or two days later after the incubation period began. A "day" is counted as a full 24 hours, so day-1 would be the first 24 hours after setting the egg, day-2 is the next 24 hours, and so on.

If you set eggs on a Monday, it's usually a safe bet that they will hatch on a Monday, 3 weeks later. Select clean, even shaped, undamaged fertilized eggs for incubating. If possible, do not store them too long pre-incubation. Ideally, eggs should be set within a week after being laid, and after ten days, the hatchability of the eggs drop significantly.

Note: All eggs supplied to you from poultry or other related sources should be allowed to rest for 24 hours prior to setting, to allow the contents of the eggs to settle. Place supplied eggs upright to settle, with the fat end of the egg in an egg carton, or something similar. Supplied eggs often have loose or damaged air cells. Before putting your eggs into an incubator, plug it in and make sure the temperature is steady. In a forced air incubator (constructed with a fan) the temperature should be 99-99.5°F. In a still air incubator, the temperature should be slightly higher, 100-101°F measured at the top of the eggs. I used a digital thermometer and a hygrometer which measures humidity in my cousin's incubators. The humidity should be within 55 to 70.

Use a non-toxic marker and mark eggs with an 'X' on one side and an 'O' on the other, this will ensure that no mistake will be made and all eggs will be turned. Remember not to wash eggs before feeding them into your incubating machine. Turn the eggs three times daily except the last 3 days because they'll start finding their ways out.

If you supply every seven into the incubating chamber (depending on your kind of construction), you will have new birds every seven days and then about another seven days will be okay to feed the newly hatched birds; and then sell the birds. This will increase the market value of the birds. If your capacity is enough you can go ahead immediately and increase your production; and hence, you may wish to move on to poultry farming if you can- OF COURSE YOU CAN!

Let me also offer the suggestion that one who has love and passion for birds procession and poultry management can also launch into birds feeds production, including eggs production.

Only Nigeria can provide one with all these opportunities, freedom, and right, even when one has not truly advanced in school towards being certified to do productions like these, and without over-taxing him. There are unlimited business opportunities in the land of Nigeria. "The man who moved a mountain was the man who began carrying away small stones." Chinese proverb.

Poultry Feeds Production

This idea is beyond some people's imagination in most instances, while many are already running the business idea to their satisfactions. It requires a grinding machine, a mixer, and a dryer; and all these machines can be locally constructed, and still fit-in for best production without breaking down.

Chicken usually eat a mixture of seeds and other goodies found around the neighbourhood. It comes in many different varieties and types, for birds of all sizes and different kinds. Some foods have very nice shapes, sizes and most times, colours to look appealing to your bird. Maybe you won't like spending a lot of money on small packages. Or maybe you just want to show off some creativity. Whatever is your reason, if you want to go into making homemade food for chicken, for marketing, or poultry consumption. This paragraph will take you a long way.

The first thing you want to do is get a drum to put your

mixture into. The size depends on how much target you wish to cover. Put some sunflower seeds in the drum (it depends on the type of food). Don't put in too many, sunflower seeds in huge quantities are not very healthy for birds. Half a bowl should do. If you are making a large amount of food, a whole bucket will work for a big drum. Add a bucket of walnuts and peanuts. If your production is for younger birds, crack and remove the shell of the peanuts and just add the middle part. Add a half bucket of dried fruit. Add a cup of dry (depending on your size of production. Consider multiplying your cup by the size of your production), hard corn, kernels. Then mix the ingredients with a long wooden stick. If it is big quantity, consider a mixer machine, and mix until everything is all scattered in the bowl/drum. When well blended and mixed, you should put it into a dryer. Store the product in a container in a cool, dry place. If you make mistake in this production process, don't worry because it will serve for pigs.

The raw materials that are used for producing of poultry feeds are grouped as follows:

(1) Cereal and grains: maize, rice, wheat, sorghum, bajra, ragi and other millets, broken rice, germs, middling and damaged wheat that is discarded from the food industry as unfit for human consumption.

(2) Cakes or Oil meal: groundnut cake, soybean meal, rapeseed meal, sesame meal, sunflower meal, coconut meal, palm meal are used as protein resources.

(3) Feed of animal origin: meat meal, fish meal, squilla meal, hatchery waste and bone meal are used. However, farmers face production problems due to bacterial contamination of fish and meat meal.

(4) By-products: rice bran, rice polish, solvent extracted rice and wheat bran, molasses and sal-seed meal

are by-products used in poultry feeds.

(5) Minerals and vitamins: poultry feeds are enriched with calcium, phosphorus, trace minerals such as Fe, Zn, Mn, Cu, CO, and I, and vitamins A, D3, E, K and B complex.

(6) Feed additives: additives commonly used are antibiotics (usage not banned in Nigeria) pre-biotic, pro-biotic, enzymes, mould inhibitors, toxin binders, anti-coccidian supplements, acidifiers, amino acids, antioxidants, feed flavours, pigments and herbal extract of Nigerian origin.

These raw materials for poultry feed production are adequately available in Nigeria. As feed cost is the key factor in determining the profitability of poultry farming, feed manufacturers as well as farmers attempt to produce least cost rations by including some of the following products, depending upon their cost, availability and nutritive value: forest produce (babul seed, rubber seed, tamarind seed, sal-seed, etc.); food industry wastes (biscuit waste, coco shell, bread waste, powder, cocoa beans, macaroni waste, skim milk powder, etc.); gum and starch industry (guar meal, tapioca, tapioca spent pulp, etc.); fruit and vegetable processing waste (citrus wastes, mango waste, tomato pomace, pineapple waste, tea leaves, etc.); alcohol industry waste (yeast sludge, grape extractions, breweries' dried grain, etc.).

Availability of raw materials has increased as the production of food grains and oil seeds in the country have risen over the past few years. Agriculture is rapidly growing in Nigeria.

The production has also increased domestic production of maize, a major ingredient in poultry feed. And it is likely to contribute to the reduction of poultry feed prices. The liberalization of feed maize production will provide a cushion for domestic production. This will help to avoid possible feed crises.

Make your right contacts to secure raw materials from your locality, and do not forget to read from a complete manual on poultry feeds production for best self utilization. Plantain chips, coconut chips, etc are all materials use in making birds' feed. Feed birds with food made in fresh fruit, pasta and bread every once in a while. These foods are okay for birds to eat and birds like to eat them too.

"Whatever you are, be a good one." - Abraham Lincoln. You are you. All that is valuable in human society depends upon the opportunity for development and civilization accorded the individuals in society. Nigeria is good. However beautiful the idea of job opportunity is, one should occasionally look at the results and achievements and consider improvement and extension. And most job opportunities are too poor for consideration and acceptance while you actually have lots of possibilities under your feet.

The most significant fact about not being an entrepreneur after schooling is that employment is the only legalized extortion of intellectual property because graduates often like to be paid. None likes to wait for too long for a business idea to mature and start yielding profits. No matter your business idea or your reasons for sorting only on a job opportunity, in this journey of successful living, "If you have the will to win, you have achieved half of your success; if you don't, you have achieved half of your failure." David Ambrose. Every dream is achievable. It is also a matter of how much courage you possess. Someone who studied electrical engineering or other related courses can start as big as electric designing, installation, and house wiring.

House Wiring

If you desire to practice electrical drawing and engineering after schooling, you may not need to register with Corporate Affairs Commission (CAC) before you can start securing contracts for yourself. But this does not mean you should not register your company to secure big contracts from government and other organizations. You can start with private individuals and contractors in your host community. And if you are not capacitance enough, you can merge with contractors, technicians and engineers who are already in the field you desire to venture. While doing so, investigate new houses in your area, or within your reach. Don't forget to consider your capacity. Do your estimation and write your contract proposal to the house owners or contractors. Put your heart, your mind, your intellect in securing the contract. If you can convince the house owner or contractor with your willpower that you have the capacity to do the job, then you have succeeded in achieving half of your success.

Keep moving. Forget yourself and start working. Go into some quiet spots. The best time for me is in bed, at night before night rest. Go to where you will not be interrupted, close your eyes and go into deep thinking about what you're passionate about if you have not really understand your passion. After you have defined clearly what your desire is, move on immediately because you can be, have or achieve thing you wishes to.

Example: Many years ago, I clearly defined my life and what I wanted in life. I want to own a mechanic workshop in years to come. I already know the capacity of the mechanic workshop I desire to operate. Sometimes, I will go to Google and read pedigrees and how to start-up the kind of mechanic workshop I desire to operate. I watch pictures and videos of engineers painting cars or running one service or the other.

I also know that I will need a job which pays me not less than N100, 000 per month for me to be able to achieve my desire after I may have worked for about ten years and above with all the rise. And, I also know that it will be better for me to work for myself and earn N50, 000 per month after balancing from expenses than to work for a company that offers me N60, 000 per month. It was painful when I was offered a job opportunity that offered to pay me N30, 000 per month, which means after balancing from expenses I would have N25, 000 or N20, 000, or even lesser to take care of transportation, medical, housing, food and so on for the month. I knew if I should earn less than N80, 000 per month it would take me about twenty-five to thirty years of work to start achieving my desire of owing a mechanic workshop. Which means I would have more life challenges, including health withdrawal, and I would not work longer before I would retire. My workshop might struggle to survive and may soon fade away.

I may not continue waiting for job opportunity which would pay me about N80, 000 per month for a start if it did not come soon. And I know I do not worth N50, 000 per month. So, I will not accept that from any employer without reasonable benefits to challenge their reasons for paying lesser. This does not mean that my wings are too high. Every man has his own worth.

I am an engineer by profession which I studied considering my desire to own and run a mechanic engineering workshop. But on the other hand, I am a passionate creative writer. So I considered my passion hence the job has not come so soon. I also studied philosophy but not in school. I know every man has more options available than he realizes. Unemployment is a total number of people without ***love*** and ***passion***.

When I published my first novel entitled ***Kingdom Far Away***, I met total setback. But the setback was not sufficient enough to strangle the passion for creative writing out of my mind. Because each time I met setback, I achieved and learned other new things I would have done. And then I kept moving because what I see in future fills my heart with joy and happiness.

Let me say it loud; ***writers, singers, comedians, graphic designers, music/movie producers, script writers*** and all other intellectuals who are on this journey of living success are secret goldmine. Without music, movies, and books life would be a big joke. If you're a writer of any calling, ***keep moving***.

Writing

If you are a creative writer, it won't be long before you will ascend onto the throne of financial freedom if you will consider it worthy to employ the BASIC PRINCIPLES OF SUCCESS explained in the previous chapter, and the LAWS OF ENDURING SUCCESS outlined in the next chapter of this handbook.

Out of my passion, I started creative writing. When I finished my first work, friends, family members and others were congratulating me. But on the other hand, some people threw in all manner of discouragement, indifferences, contempt, and fear. Most of them told me that ***writing*** will not feed me in Nigeria. Most of them simply asked me, "What else do you do? You won't make a living in writing." But they did not tell me I could actually offer my book to universities, polytechnics, colleges, and other institutions of learning. Most of them explained to me how it would take years for government to review my book for secondary schools. Nobody told me I could actually sell my book worldwide on Amazon. When I eventually took my book into the markets, especially schools, they accepted it. I did self publishing, so I retained all the copyrights. Most of my friends and family members were angry that I had rejected a job that offered me N30,000 per month, which I would have to work from 7am to 5pm every day, including on Sundays, depending on workshift. That was not the way I planned it. They didn't tell me that my books alone are insufficient for all the schools in one state, let lone Nigeria as a nation, and then other countries. That it would all depend on how many schools I could secure to review and recommend my book.

I can happily hand over distribution rights to distributors at any cost I so wish. It is now and always a matter of what I think and want. God made man chief-in-command of the materials within his mind. If you are a creative writer and you have one lecturer in any school, you are blessed. If you don't have, you are more blessed because you won't know when you will push your writing career beyond your capacity in most instances. Do it, it's all right with GOD. I once recruited eight salespersons from different schools when it became necessary that I had to make a loan payment. I gave them copies of my book and allowed them opportunity to make fifty naira per copy. But they each returned back every two or three days to request for more copies. Because I used posters of my book to decorate walls around their school premises. That way, I sold four hundred and six copies of ***Kingdom Far Away*** in twenty-six days, and I became famous to a certain level.

"In life, in a football game, the principle is hit the ball hard." Roosevelt. If you leave your talent and wait for employment opportunity, your talent will leave you and hide in lack of willpower and self-confidence. If you leave your plan and go for work, your plan will leave you and go for work. In life, whatever good thing one accomplishes will end up building him.

People never ask a man who is a failure what are the principles of failure. It is boldly written and no man wants to fail in life. Why then does no man want to consider the basic principles of success? Nobody is born to fear and fail. All man are born free, yet entangled by negative thinking and lack of adequate knowledge. There is no such fact like evil spirits being in power. When a person goes to church and a man of God tells him that an evil spirit from his mother's or father's race has been hindering him from making progress, getting promotion in his workplace, getting employment, and so on, the person should not worry. Prophecy is nothing but just an estimation based on one's irregularities of life. Your progress and prosperity are guaranteed by God from the beginning of creation. Evil spirit is an affair of the mind which is like smoke that will vanish away once the living fire begets cold ashes. This expression may also help you to understand that when the devil came to steal from man (men and women), kill the inner man, and destroy man (men and women), Jesus also came that man (men and women) may have life in abundance. This expression is made to help understand that when poverty came, prosperity also came; when darkness came, light also came; when sickness came, healing also came; when failure came, success also came. Man may carry in him some certain level of knowledge and read books on secrets of prosperity and Spiritual Laws so well that he begins to understand the nature of humanity. And once that happens, his willpower will begin to overpower the negative forces in his mind that all the negative spirits will flee. He will begin to see all the ways which he has violated the commandment of the principles of prosperity which has hindered him from being prosperous. That is just in literature- books. Only books can empower the mind and drive away bad spirits as such. Movies and music do not have the power to do that. No man is created to be inferior. But "Lack of knowledge (of Spiritual Laws), people perish." Holy Bible. When you fill your mind with such words like, "***I am not unemployed***", "***I can achieve success in my career***", "***I am successful***", "***my dream cannot die***", the bad spirits which cause bad feelings and low self-esteem will feel insecure and leave without saying good bye. And only then will you begin to realize the options available to you to find your route to successful living. Follow the foregoing instructions in its fullness and it will open the way for a complete understanding and mastery of the principles of living success.

Every employable graduate who wants to venture into soap making is on the right track to a lucrative business idea.

Soap Making

Many people make the mistake of assuming that, because I'm the one producing this item, it may not be well received. Therefore they usually settle for less quality and never press hard. You are wrong. Every production can reach its highest selling point. It's only a matter of what you think and want. Detergents which are recorded to be among the top ten of the daily consumed items in every household can get to any length, into any hands and with any speed. The questions are, "How much of willpower have you put in?", "What are your marketing strategies?", "How good are your products?" It is not about having more or little schooling, or about having acquired a certificate in marketing department without adequate knowledge, because if it is, there won't be failure.

During my research study on '***Performance of a Product*** in the marketplace, I realized that the performance of any product in the market may depend on many factors such as, "Availability of the products to final consumers", "Power of attractive packaging", "How many people know about the products", "What is the value-cost of the product? this includes cost and quality", and so on. Once you are able to solve these factors, you will understand how it promotes the income level of every manufacturer. Only then, are you ready to bargain with life in manufacturing. Detergent manufacturing is one business idea any one should consider to venture into. It requires you to know the use of caustic soda, perfume, soda ash, colorant, silicate or starch, glazerol and so on. Consider advancing your knowledge with the help of a complete manual on soap production. Try to consider colour choice and perfume because it is halfway to achieve market success. This same thing applies to catering and bakery business. When you consider interior decoration and cake making, you may also want to extend your mind to exterior decoration too. Yet underwear, male ties, female designers' belts made in local fabric are also choices to consider.

Interior Decoration

One can spend four to five years of study to end up lesser than an interior decorator. Yet many people think that interior decoration is not worth venturing into. Verily I tell you, gold is gold everywhere. Many philosophers have made the statement that man is the master of his own earthly destiny. You, as a master, should learn to apply like a master in all walks of life. It is not enough for one to wait until one is contracted to decorate before one can do something. Bukky Bello did not misunderstand this business idea. She was just passionate about it. Having the knowledge of interior decoration, catering and bakery can keep you growing rapidly.

In every business idea, understand that concentration is a must. Whether you wish to conduct effectively your daily affairs of life, or to succeed financially, or if your goal is spiritual, you need to concentrate to the positive will. Many graduates make the mistake of misunderstanding their power of spoken word and its acceptance. It is good to be careful with what you say, what you listen to, and what you accept. Man, knowing the power of spoken word should be careful of his confessions. He has only to watch the reaction of his words to know that they do not return void. Through power of spoken word, man is continually making *laws* for himself. Firstly, do not make the mistake of accepting the fallacy that there is no job opportunity in the land available for you. This way, your mind will nurse you as a potential employee if it's employment you seek, and there will be a rising self confidence each time you go for job interview. Secondly, do not make the mistake of accepting negative things people say to you, for most people have not work harder than you have done. During my National Youth Service orientation course, most corps members interpreted NYSC for '***Now Your Suffering Continues***'. These were the sixty percent of people whose mind had already failed, they knew they were going to suffer for they had lacked sufficient knowledge. One with sincere positive mind would have said "***Now Your Success Continues***". These were people who may have suffered setback in one area of life and they did no longer believe there was a brighter life after schooling. They were the sixty percent of people whose subconscious mind were no longer ready. There is unlimited right extended to people with more or little schooling, and limited tax and revenue to be paid. Only a country like Nigeria can provide such rights to people with insufficient education or certificate to practice, or to venture into business ideas and acquire wealth to any possible height without restriction from government.

I am still waiting for somebody to come up with an idea on how to develop application software of Holy Bible and Holy Koran into audio application software materials. Application software which will be installed in a computer system and be operated in a method similar to the way one accesses an audio compact disk. It will enable men of God to reduce the time spent reading verse to verse. It will enable a blind man to also make use of the Holy Bible or Holy Koran. This means that everyone can get closer in knowing Spiritual Laws. It would be in a platform in which one chapter will have the rest of the verses sublisted like an audio tracks. It will enable a quicker conversion and help downgrade the factors bringing sins and violation of laws to mankind.

Let me propose a way. Employ the service of a music producer, software programmer and readers (similar to broadcasters). The software programmer does the programming in such a segment that every books of the Holy Bible and Holy Koran will appear on the computer screen. The producer will record the readers as they read from the book after which they will upload it to the software.

Let any investor consider a complete research and analysis on this classic idea. I know it's achievable. There is gold everywhere in the land, even beneath your feet. All you have to do is to keep digging. Do not let people influence your thinking. In reality, riches do not come to a man as a result of formal education. Because, every graduate is a man of formal education but it is not certain that every graduate will be rich. Yet, every rich man, in sincerity of truth, is a man of knowledge, with more or little formal education.

Poverty is not a reality. It is a fact number of people born crippled, without hearing means, without hands, without parents or family members, then later lost mind - insanity. I have never heard of such a man. I never heard of poverty. Those who are unsuccessful usually make the mistake of thinking and believing they need an additional schooling. The truth is that, schooling provides only but little of the practical knowledge required for one to develop from within and prepare one's mind to acquire anything one wants without passing ill-feelings to others. If you decide to take additional education to improve your knowledge, to what purpose?, If the purpose for which you want the knowledge you seek is to acquire practical knowledge that is related to your major purpose, business, or advancing your talent, then consider a reliable source. Education does not truly end in school, for practical education begins ***after schooling***, in the real world. How saddening it is that after all these tumultuous years of schooling, a graduate will be locked down in his bedroom all in the name of unemployment. All successful man, of all calling, have approved that accumulation of wealth begins in a prepared mind, not as a result of successful schooling, therefore keep moving.

Six

Attain And Endure Success

Staying successful is actually a problem facing most people in employment, in business, and in all other careers. They don't teach people the principles of enduring success in school. You wait for opportunity to knock and it did not. You break the door and seize opportunities, yet you fail again. You don't understand life. It doesn't seem to make sense to rise again. But there's no joy living your whole life on the ground.

Now I tell you, the problem of man is of man. It is obvious that financial depression and lack of inner peace brought over 500, 000 candidates to the very borderline of unknown fate during Nigeria Immigration Service recruitment exercise. They misunderstood the forces which are unseen, the forces which brought justice to man and regulate his condition. Most of them with limited knowledge of this regulation sought to turn up for the recruitment exercises on 15th March, 2014, in a sense to improve their living. Understand that the whole number which turned up for the recruitment exercise was not the true reflection of unemployed youths in the land of Nigeria.

Through the ages which have passed, most of them have depended so much on their conventional knowledge, and have limited their belief to education they acquired in institution of learning. They have now entered the most magnificent institution of all ages- real life. The whole number which reflected at the screening centres had not the capacity to understand the natural law of prosperity and financial skills, and obey it, in order to make a living and sustain funds from their places of work or businesses.

Most of them were thinking of security instead of opportunity. They seemed to be more afraid of death than life. Man, with all his level of education and mixed culture, has failed to understand that success is a matter of a simple mind and cannot be determined merely by the amount of money and material possessions you have. More money has always come with more spending. "Be bold and mighty forces will come to your aid." - Basil King. Success goes beyond and deeper than how much you're being paid monthly or how much money you achieved in a one straight business endeavour. It could be measured by the extent to which your inner peace and mental control enables you to be in command of all circumstances while obeying your inner audience. That is success in reality. It is not what we have acquired but the attention be given to whom we have become. The naturally developed secret is an inside job. To be very precise, there is just one problem with seeing success as job opportunity or how much one is being paid monthly. It is not that job, talent and good plans will not help one stay in success, rather, success is as a result of many factors and applied laws. ***Our culture, efforts of parents, our environments, our attitudes, our emitted efforts, good friends, efforts of leaders, the lesions of life, family members***, all these and many more contribute to success and to endure success. In the light of this statement, Jim Ryun, for the sole purpose of carrying out physical examination on human behaviour, says that "Motivation is what gets you started. Habit is what keeps you moving."

However, I encourage you to concentrate your mind. The first foundation of success is ***desire***, while the second foundation is ***concentration***. You're obligated to channel all your energies to one worthy point, and to go directly to that point, looking neither to the right, nor to the left till you soon reach the end. Understand that ability to follow the course of one examined business idea to become successful is the test for every successful entrepreneur. To remain focused. How you make use of these momentum principles of life will determine how you will succeed. This statement is also made upon the very understanding that, "Most people give up just when they're about to achieve success. They quit on the one yard line. They give up at the last minute of the game, one foot from a winning touchdown." - Ross Perot. That is a big issue with most people because they do not visualize. They do not have vision which is the only ability to see into the future. They neither love what they do, nor believe in what they do, and then it becomes complicated.

Example: Most of the youths who turned up on 15th of March, 2014 for employment exercises at Nigeria Immigration Service recruitment centres were in business while some of them were employed. It seemed reasonable to me when I made my summary on the research as regards their exact reasons, and discovered that they met setbacks which will always be met, and then they found it difficult to move ahead financially which they should for they lack financial intelligence. They could not succeed in their jobs or businesses because they lack the knowledge of the **Basic Principles of Success** and **Financial Skills**. Then they sought to change course. It is not about wishing to stop, to combine, or to switch over from one job opportunity or business to the other. But this does not mean you will have to remain lagging in an unexamined business idea.

Every man is successful and becomes what he has by the law he obeys. In the arrangement of his **desire**, man is anxious to improve his career, business or job performance and endure success, but he is not persistently willing to improve himself so he remained bound and stagnant. To become successful and endure success, there is no limit to things you will stake.

There was a man who went to a food restaurant to eat. He made his order and while his food was being prepared, he changed his order and made a different order. Just after another three minutes, he changed his order again. But he was very hungry and he became angry. He then complained "*What is holding back my order?* This man was the reason why his food was delayed being served and the stress his supplier went through because he didn't stick to his first order. Most men are like that. They are as rigid as iron and unyielding as bronze. Accept that habit can make you lag in life. There is really no limit or shortage in the world. Wrong and negative words are only but powerful enemies. By the law of his being, man is magnified. This statement is as true as the sky being lightly blue. Those who are out of harmony with their surroundings, jobs or businesses should be content that life is really bigger than man's ego and can supply more than man can demand. The desire in man comes to him as a response of the inner spirit because he demand and believe. Put it at the back of your mind that no man is holding down your own fortune. Every one who is ready to pay the price, to obey the principles of prosperity will be prosperous. And to endure success, you need to concentrate your energies at your strongest flashy points. You gain more by finding a rich goldmine and mining it deeper than by flitting from one shallow mine to another. When deep economic changes occur and business is slacking, new strategies designed to work in a changing business climate are required. Remain focused. Just because one successfully started a business or is gainfully employed does not mean you will endure success. You need to put in more effort and time. Always be on the look out for opportunity to improve your work performance or business productivity, and make it stand out of competition. If you're a marketer or a distributor and downturn is still churning, do a better research analysis and find out what your clients and customers really want from you and do your best to get them what they need. You need to also be careful about offering too much discount on a product because doing so could devalue your brands, products or services after the downturn is over.

There is an uncertainty in economic community which is affecting everyone's job, business, and the world at large. These uncertainties are the one creating social, mental, psychological, and financial stress on everyone. Owing to these uncertainties, enduring success depends on how flexible one is. Good successful business owners may lose their tracks in business for once or twice times, but somehow they employ flexibility and overcome the setbacks and resume their relentless progress.

For many months, I made my research on performance of a product in the marketplace and what distinguishes companies that perform at a very high level over a very long period from the other companies that do not perform as well. To solve this matrix, I did all the business analysis. I selected few companies that have turned in an extraordinary high performance over the past few years. I also went through corporate histories, read some person's pedigrees and considered some fundamentals principles all of them had employed. And I found out that the greatest companies and successful individuals who still maintain high grade in financial trace-back over their investments do not excel through radical innovation, daring transformation and downturn except they adapt to the constant changing business environment by being knowledgeable and intelligently conservative. They naturally apply what I call "***The Twenty-Two Laws of Enduring Success***". These laws are the mandate which carries them through all the uncertainty of economy in job or business community. While there is no guarantee that the companies and individuals whom I have studied will never fall on hard times. I only considered and believed that there is much to learn from their business strategies, histories, and personal pedigrees.

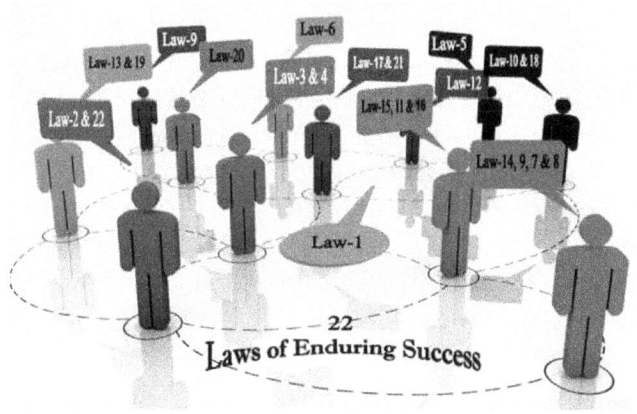

THE TWENTY-TWO LAWS OF ENDURING SUCCESS

Law One
Recreate Yourself

"The Year You Leave School Marks Only Your Entry Into The Real World. Henceforth, Other Years Will Be Different From Your Former Life" **Ekeh Joe Obinna**

This is actually where your job begins immediately after schooling in order to become successful and endure success. You need to assume the characteristics of a successful master. This assumption is an inside job. It only means to work on your mind (inner man) and consider your thoughts and spoken words. Your thought is your foundational key to actions which often lead you to success. No wonder the Holy Bible makes the same expression. Recreation is a true ***authority*** given to man from the day of creation. *"Do not conform yourselves to the standards of this world, but let God transform you inwardly by a complete change of your 'mind. Then you will be able to know the will of God- what is good, perfect and is pleasing to him."* - Romans 12 vs 2; Good News Bible.

Little by little the truth is being unfolded that it all begins in the mind. Until it now appears to certain people, including Robert Greene, the author of **'The 48 Laws of Power'** who understood this law when he says *"Do not accept the roles that society foists on you. Recreate yourself by forging a new identity, one that commands attention and never bores the audience. Be the master of your own image rather than letting others define it for you. Incorporate dramatic devices into your public gestures and actions your willpower will be enhanced and your character will seem larger than life."*

When you recreate yourself (that is, purify your mind) you will no longer be limited by troubles of life. All problems come with an unidentified solution to it. You will know when your mind lulls you into inaction when there is climate change in business community. You will know how to improve your thoughts and what to think about at all given situations. It means you can boast your confidence and your job performance. It will help you decide how to control your mental state during your daily actions. People who refuse to take chances in business have not been listening to their minds, because they fear criticism which may come to them from people around them if they fail. If you relieve your mind of wrong clusters and adopt positive thinking as a way of life, it will bring constructive changes which will make you happier, brighter and more successful. You will know what desire your mind has generated for you and how to follow it once you listen to your inner audience.

With a positive thinking attitude, you meet the brighter side of life. You'll become optimistic, and expect the best to happen. It is certainly a state of mind that will manifest creative thinking and optimism. The motivation and energy to do things and accomplish goals will also be enhanced. It will help in many ways such as:

? Expecting success and not failure,

? Making you feel inspired,

? Giving you the strength not to give up should you encounter obstacles on your way,

? Making you regard failures and problems as blessings in disguise,

? Helping you believe in yourself and in your abilities,

? Making you have more self-esteem and self-confidence,

? Helping you look for solutions, instead of dwelling in

problems,

? Helping you see and recognize opportunities, and so on.

All these are as a result of state of the mind. The essential point of purifying your mind is because you need to understand that liberation from suffering cannot be found outside the state of mind. Man is the product of his mind's condition. Permanent liberation can only be found by purifying the mind. Therefore, if man wants to become free from problems and attain lasting peace, happiness, and success, he needs to increase the purification of his mind and be in harmony with his inner audience.

Law Two
Fashion Weapon From What Nature Provides

"Everything You Can Imagine Is Real." - **Pablo Picasso**

If you have no desired life to accomplish, there is nothing to work for and achieve. If you do set goals, that means, being on a journey of success, your weapon to overcome challenges is not the infrastructures you see around you, but your mind. Your mind is your natural armoury where you will fashion weapon and deal with procrastination, lack of interest, indecision, fear of failure, indifferences, weakness, including the habit of blaming others for your shortcomings. All the enemies one meet on one's road to success are always an affair of the subconscious mind. They generally exist only in the mind. If you win in your mind, you win in your life. Take yourself into account and determine in what particular way, if any of these traits is overpowering you.

Countless others have come and gone, many generations have gone, but the treasures in the land remain unlimited.

Imagination is everything. *One way to fashion weapon from nature is to refuse deliberately to do, think or say the wrong, negative, and unnecessary things*. Naturally, things one says or thinks has power to influence one's habit and behaviour, including one's visualization which coins from mental image. Man should consider a goal and set on a journey, because all he needs is within him. Most people, however, are in ignorance of their natural weapon, and they do not really know their true desire. They are striving for things and situations which do not belong to them and such would only bring failure and dissatisfaction in their lives if attained. These people have not recreated themselves and do not know their destinations.

Your weapon is your imagining faculty which must be trained and used without violating the natural law guiding these principles. When a person violates the natural law guiding the principles of one's imagining faculty, we often see that person bring into his life every unrighteous desire of his heart sickness, hatred, failure, wrong self expression, making enemies, lack of self-worth, bad influence, and so on. To use the natural weapon, man must recreate himself to understand the working of his mind positively. "Human beings can alter their lives by altering their attitudes of the mind." William James.

Law Three
No Hand Should Stand Idle

"*There Is Gold Everywhere*" - **Robert Kiyosaki**

In life, not everyone is trained to be successful, but everyone is created to be bold and succeed. To become successful and endure success, *no hand should stand idle*. Most men and women still think and believe in the philosophy of trying to receive without giving. They want to earn some benefits without working. Most of them are government workers. Some of them are using someone else's certificates to sustain their jobs. They refused to be trained or acquire education towards being certified to be usefully employed. Some of these men and women demand for little work time and more pay. Others do not take the trouble of working at all, they are ghost workers. Most of them are on the internet seeking whom to defraud. Others are directors and secretaries who create ghost workers who do not exist at all in government organizations to get more pay. Their idea is that they are using what they have to get what they want - they are being brilliant and smart. I am not unmindful that most of them have entered into the real world unprepared and are facing great trials and tribulations of modern life. It's all right. But the pure knowledge is lacked. If you are one of those who still believe that riches can be attained by mere organizing of an idea to rub money without giving an equivalent service, or you're a ghost worker, or you are one of those men and women who demands for more pay for inferior products or little services you offer, if you are one of those who stands their hands idle, trying to receive monetary benefits without giving the seed of an equivalent, if you are one of those who violates the ***natural principles of prosperity***, you manipulate, pirate or imitate an existing products in the market community- producing fake items. Verily I tell you, as great as you may seem, as comfortable as you may feel about your formula, that idea or method does not, and can never bring riches and wealth in reality. No successful living come a man who has not emitted an equivalent effort. There is only one dependable way of acquiring wealth and becoming financially buoyant and that is by rendering an equivalent service or selling an equivalent products/items. **Nature made this principle**. Man is to continue working with the faith that unearned service is redemptive. What you give, you must receive.

There is no way you can look healthy without supplying to your body an equivalent supplements which you may desire its outlook. Accept that "Striving for success without hard work is like trying to harvest where you haven't planted." David Bly. "I tell you, there is only one way of receiving anything and that is by giving it everything." Scott Alexander. This is the basic rule of ***living success***. You must give in order to receive, work in order to earn freely. Now, go back to work, knowing that success can, and will be attained sincerely.

This is more than a theory. It is a natural promise that anyone whose hands do not stand idle but gives must receive the seed of an equivalent. Remember this **'law'** always. It is more important than a liquid capital of any business idea or monthly salary of any job opportunity. It is above and beyond the control, manipulation, and influences of both **human beings** and **machines**. One's financial continuation depends upon how one respects this principle.

Law Four
Stand Your Thoughts Toward Future

"I Am Yet To Hear A Man Ask For Advice On How To Proceed From What Lies Behind Us To Get What Lies Before Us." - **Ekeh Joe Obinna**

Pains and sorrows are the conditions of man in a complicated life. There is no successful business or an entrepreneur that has not tasted the bitterness of setback. If it is riches you seek, do not overlook the possibility of a goal you would have reached if you didn't meet setback. That goal is still there waiting for you to regain bearing and set on. Upon the understanding of the power of the mind, your future grows out of every single thought you hold in your mind. There is no way, and I speak with gladness, by which business environment can be slain of challenges forever.

Following the inmost desire, it is very necessary to stand every single thought towards future. No man comes to harmony with a peaceful tomorrow if he does not build a way today in a simple thought and allows his thoughts to influence his actions. If he solely desires wealth and riches, let him at every evening think about, as many as he can imagine, of what he desires to do in future. Write them down if he so wish. While he falls asleep his subconscious mind will work on them, on the best ways for him to achieve them. Then, the next day will conform a brighter day.

Nature is the art of God, it has made man plain and simple, free to rise as high as he's able and willing to; and the degree to which he stands his thoughts determines the degree he would reach. Do not waste time thinking backwards. And always prepare for the days when things will not go as well as they are going now. If you are rendering service to people, put it in mind that a certain or particular client may not remain loyal forever, and do not make the mistake of thinking that a certain territory is all wrapped up. If you're a salesperson, there is no limit to the kind of designs and other challenging products you may see in the marketplaces. Even if you have produced quality products or services to people in the past, you must stand your thoughts towards future and show that you can and will always continue to do so tomorrow and the day after. That is a way to make clients and customers depend on you and your products. The more you are relied on, the more independent you are. It is only when you stand your thoughts towards future that you will enjoy immunity, and will always be able to provide enough in time for your clients and customers.

Law Five
Never Let No One Know How Much You Own

"If Pains Were Romance, Then My Envious Friends And Jealous Neighbours Are Very Romantic." - **Ekeh Joe Obinna**

When you are on top, there is envy. The wealthier you are, the more trouble people will create for you, and want to make you vulnerable. It is good to show less than necessary. Only the minds of envious friends and jealous neighbours are enough of bad instrument to attract setbacks, challenges, and opposition to you when you, man as a spiritual being, is on the journey of living success. In all calling, successful men always go through the un-constructed narrow road to living success being in competition with no one. Always remember this. It will gravitate you to apply Law-14 of ***enduring success***. You may work as a team but know it's a personal race with different destinations. Keep people's attention off balanced and always away from you when the level of your wealth is the issue by never revealing to them the level of your success and financial fitness. If they have no knowledge of what you have acquired they will not prepare to compete or outshine you. They will betray you more easily because of envy and jealousy if you show superior over them.

In business community, failure is an agony familiar to most men and women who fall on hard times of challenges that come from envious friends, neighbours, and jealous family members. Always make those around you feel more comfortably superior whenever the level of acquired wealth is the issue. In your desire to succeed, do not show too much talent or wealth. Wise, brilliant, and safe is the man who shows less for more to protect the incoming wealth, and such a man will attain success.

Law Six
Let God Who Leads You Guide You

"The Churches Have Failed. The Mosques Have Also Failed. Households Are Not Helpful. But Society Is Trying, It Has Succeeded In Shaping The Duration OF Every Man." - **Ekeh Joe Obinna**

Why have youths grown old in an unprepared mind? Most have gone ritually unclean, like making bad blood in order to acquire wealth and riches. It is because they have left the source of their strength and insights. No man has ever seized the sources of treasure in the land. Those who acquired, acquired too few and can be counted. Others have come along to take their places.

On the journey of successful living, to become rich and acquire wealth, man is a spiritual being. His mind is on an invisible un-constructed road to acquire the desire of his heart. There is no way to measure how wide, how large, or the boundaries of wealth man can acquire. Man may sail across seas to find the desires of his heart, but there is a spirit guiding him. Be it a white or black spirit, it exist within the borderline of his mind.

Upon this understanding, the spirit which you believe in, which you were made of His likeness and image is required to construct the invisible road and lead you through it.

When man violates the ***Spiritual Laws*** guiding him, he becomes limited to a certain level of living success, depending on the level of violation. And now, he will have to work double to attain and accomplish his simple journey. Firstly, he will work harder than he would in order not to violate the principles again. And secondly, he will task himself to work to accomplish his heart desire on his own due to lesser grace from the Spirit that guides him. During man's limitations, while suffering to acquire his heart desire, man understands that his soul suffers more than his body. This is because the body obeys the movements of the soul. "Plain and simple we were made but complicated we have made everything."- Ecclesiastes 7:29.

God is man's supplier. And only he who knows your abundance of wealth can lead you to it. Churches, on the other hand, have today, failed to teach man *Spiritual Laws*. Man does not, and cannot conform himself to the standard of spiritual requirements based upon hearing of mere statements but upon knowledge and understanding of such spiritual requirements. Owing to lack of knowledge and understanding of **Spiritual Laws**, most men and women have continued to find it very difficult to acquire wealth and become rich even upon repentance and salvation because they keep violating the laws which judge and guide them since they are unknown to them. Man ought to know that he's the one who keeps the name of Almighty God alive. It is not sufficient to say, 'I have repented, therefore I should be successful'. Yes, you are right, but not without harmonizing with laws of prosperity. Hence, "My people are doomed because they do not acknowledge me," Hosea 4:6 Good News Bible.

The knowledge and expression of Spiritual Laws brings man in harmony with the understanding of principles of prosperity, principles of salvation and repentance, power of love, power of spoken word, power of faith and hope and so on. This means, riches and wealth is acquired as a result of knowledge. Salvation is achieved as a result of knowledge and obedience to Spiritual Laws. It is same expression as to say there will be love, good health, faith and hope, and sickness is overcome, affliction is calmed. All these will come as a result of acquired knowledge of Spiritual Laws.

In business community, there is a 'command' that promises success. Obey the command and you'll be successful. God is everywhere in every religion; in every mind of those who require, in truth and in spirit, the guidance of He who exists only in the mind of every countryman on earth, to lead them to their abundance of wealth due to them by His grace as man may also require.

Law Seven
Plan All The Way To The End

"In Every Conceivable Manner, My Plan Is A Link Born From My Abilities, Bridge To My Future, Till A Lasting Journey." - **Ekeh Joe Obinna**

I take it that what all man is really seeking is some form of, perhaps only a plan or formula to achieve inner peace and living success. If you have passion for a talent or a hobby, and you will like to make it your profession. No matter how enthusiastic you are about your passion for the unborn business idea, it won't be successful unless you have a plan in place of how you're going to start and run it. It doesn't matter how long or detailed your plan is, as long as it covers a few essential points from the beginning to the end. Nurture your mind with great plans and thoughts, for you will never grow any higher than you plan and think.

A single talent and gifted hand is not sufficient immunity to failure in life. It must be nurtured on a daily basis and on a straight line of a careful plan and pursued to the end. Aside from your strategy, there are also priorities for other factors of your business idea like growth, management, and financial health. Use your plan to set a foundation for these factors, and then do revise as the business evolves. You're obligated to keep track of what needs to happen and in what order.

For an example: If you have to schedule a product release to match customers' demand or services to match a standard, your business management advice may be invaluable in keeping you organized and on track. Use your business plan to keep track of dates and deadlines in one place. This is essential even for sole proprietorship (one person business) and also vital for teams (a complete business organization).

Having a business plan gives you a way to be proactive and not reactive about your business idea. Do not wait for things to happen, you need to plan them. Follow up by tracking the results and making course corrections. It's a myth that your business plan is supposed to predict the future. Instead, it sets expectations and establishes assumptions so you can manage the future with course corrections.

Robert Greene also made this discovery when he says, "The ending is everything. Plan all the way to it, taking into account all the possible consequences, obstacles, and twists of fortune that might reverse your hard work and give the glory to others. By planning to the end, you will not be overwhelmed by circumstances and you will know when to stop. Gently guide fortune and help determine the future by thinking far ahead."

The majority of people are ready to come on board of the sailing ship and throw in their business plans and aims, and then forget to prepare for possible misfortunes. Most of them move on despite all opposition, they persist. If one wants to talk about people who have been heroes over deliberate journeys of success in one area or the other, one should not forget to mention that such people's back-up plans introduced their plans to the end.

Law Eight
Leave A Backup Plan Behind

"The Best Place To Solve A Problem Is On Paper." - **Jim Robin**

"In order to succeed you must fail so that you know what not to do the next time."- Anthony J. D'Angelo. Every one will realize his dream if he **keeps moving**. Be it a lucrative job, substantial business, nice house, good cars, or financial freedom. You may have a hobby you wish to turn into source of income, or maybe you are gifted with a talent you wish to develop and use to achieve your financial freedom, simply do it for love.

I wish I can simply tell you that to become successful is an easy thing. But, it's not. For those of us who went through difficult trails and years of discouragement, when *fear* was our breakfast and there was no *solid* hope, all of us who failed, not once, will not forget how we failed countless times. We will not wait for that to happen again. We leave a backup plan behind because we do not wish to go through such experiences of delay in life again. With the help of a BACKUP PLAN, you can shape your character and circumstances, and there will no longer be delay to rise again after you meet setback. This statement is not made upon mere observation, it came as a result of years of unemployment, dark days of self-denial, sacrifices, failures and unaware challenges of life which brought about self-education and carefully arranged analysis of most successful men and women who have attained success in attracting opportunities to themselves and also in attracting things they may have desired.

Too many employees fail to write a business plan. This little matrix keeps a lot of people from the benefit of good management and business success. It's hard to stick to a strategy through the daily routine and interruptions without a business plan. Use a business plan to summarize the main points of your strategy and when the routine gets corrupt, the need for your backup plan will simply manifest.

My years of failures disclosed the knowledge that backup plan will prepare your subconscious mind, which controls your behaviour and reaction during setback. It is the same expression that failure is never final.

A lot of people have ideas and great plans, but there are few who decide to do something about their great plans now. Such do not wait till tomorrow, not next week or when setback comes, but today. Those are the true over comers. These true over-comers have great plans to achieve their desires and greater plans to move on when they meet setback.

Understand that this *law* simply mean to express that the force which is in harmony with success can be supreme over failure when there is a greater force acting in parallel for a second chance. Keep moving. This force will succeed in shaping the duration of your time management and achievement. Success will come to the man who never fails to rise again upon adoption of his backup plan, because the journey of successful living has no end at last. No wonder why Babe Ruth says "You just can't beat the person who never gives up."

Law Nine
Never Alter The Proper Time

"The Man Who Moved A Mountain Was The One Who Began To Carry Away Small Stones." - **Chinese Proverb**

Most people are still trying to manage their lives with the same outdated conventions that their parents and grandparents used decades ago.

There is a noticeable big difference between **Time Management** and **Achievement**. You may delay but time will never. If you obey the principle guiding the movement of time- that is doing things at the right time, you won't have to work harder. I have sincerely devoted a month and half to study the philosophy of 'Time' and 'Achievement', and I have here analyzed the economic advantages of good time management through which individuals can accumulate fortunes in whatever amount they may have desired. Here, I captured the **law** which presents the answers to the questions such as:

"How did it get too late so soon?",

"How do I stop the time so as to stop myself from getting old?",

"What is not better than being late?"

This is the greatest subconscious equalizer among us all. We all have the same twenty-four hours per day as others do. Millions of men and women throughout the neighbourhood and around the world still engage in old convention of working harder (without a proper plan) so as to achieve their desire before they get old. They try to take one day at a time but several days attack them at once. They are right. They have exchanged the **'principles of success'** for working **'harder'** than they should. Most of them still think it is better not to retire. They always wish to stop time. If you are one of those who think that riches can be attained by spending your time to wait for job opportunity which you have come to believe that it's the only starting degree for your financial success, if you are one of those who still think that working **_harder_** is the only answer to success, your idea is that you don't want to lose time as time is money. You may rest securely on your idea, with certain knowledge that it's a personal race. But we are living in a whole new convention now. It's time to put your life to work in a proper way and proper time. Time is the only constraint. It may not be today that anything can be impossible but maybe in a lifetime to come hereafter. There are people who may no longer be able to adopt the cash flow guideline. These are the sixty percent of people who were unprepared for financial trouble at the early stage of life. Though they were gainfully employed, they mismanaged proper time. Now they are still employees whose salaries are not sufficient to handle whole family financial challenges.

But, the big question is " _When is not the proper time?_ " Do not make the mistake of not starting your dream business or not to start achieving your desired lives when you have the chance and time. You only have one _life_ and one _time_, use them now. Your life cannot be repeated. Make up your mind on time. There is nothing as powerful as a made-up mind. Do not give yourself another excuse to put off making up your mind. Time will not wait for you.

How many assets or how much cash do you have right now? Probably, your assets plus cash at hand plus your savings plus inheritance are not even worth N500, 000. In other words, you don't have much to lose right now. And you think that even if you should lose them, you still have many years ahead to recover. Wrong! No man can be above the **_Law of Time_**.

Start today, get on the journey and take all the rational and well-calculated risks to achieve your life goals. Every employable graduate owes it to the world, to his nation, to his family and most importantly, to himself; to live a life of fulfilment.

Law Ten
Keep Moving

"Success Is A Journey, Not A Destination." - **Arthur Ashe**

Too many people have refused to set goals. They are afraid to start careers because they fear environmental traits, or maybe criticism that will come from friends or family members. They simply fear to fail. If you are one of those who wait for government to create real jobs, you are in trouble. You have to understand that there are so many ways of moving forward but only one way of standing still. If you are one of those employees who sought their job security only, you hope highly in becoming a highly paid employee. Now you wish to go back to school to acquire more certificates because you want promotion- your financial strength can no longer account for your expenses. You are one of the 30 percent of people with low income and high expenses. Your plight was demonstrated in The Nation Newspaper on 5th Feb, 2013.

Are you one of those who fear losing money over a business idea but now you blame someone else for your financial downturn? Look at many graduates who have failed simply because they were programmed by school system to focus in getting a paid job in their area of specialization. They were neither taught how to follow another path nor taught how to develop and expand. But they know that becoming a company owner truly exists.

I cringe whenever I hear a graduate ask "What kind of business idea can someone like me really adopt?" There are lots of business ideas any employable Nigerian graduate can adopt. In this 21st century, no employable graduate should go home wretched. I will name a few of such business ideas, but, you must be cautioned to consider your passion and desire. Your God-given business idea may not fall within these few ideas listed. *(All lucrative business ideas cannot be accommodated herein)*

Graphic designing (to include website designing)
Poultry farming (to include feed production)
Soap making, Air Fresheners, Perfumes, etc
Fish farming
Construction (to include machines designing)
Egg Production, Pig Farming
Financial Agency (to include lending funds)
Writing, Dancing, Acting, etc
Auto Power Change-over, Inverter, Security Camera, etc (design and installation)
Manufacturing (nylon bags, paper, tissue-paper, school chalks, etc)
Bottle / Sachet Water Production
Learning institutions (Nursery School and Day Care is lucrative)
Catering and Bakery
Exterior and Interior decoration (to include sewing of males and females underwear, ties, making of female belts with local fabrics, etc)

After Schooling, the first commandment is to '***recreate yourself***' and '***keep moving***', to focus on a career even if you're employed. Everybody benefits from a society of ambitious over-achievers who never stopped wondering 'what do I do next?' The troubles arising from man's endeavour to earn a living, to find love, hope, courage, contentment and inner peace are all problems of life. The question now is "What to do next?" as well as "How to do it?" and until this matrix is solved, a lot of graduates are already a long way gone to being delayed in life; while some will fall into the dry hands of wretchedness and financial depression.

During business depressions, Intercontinental Bank Plc acquired Equity Bank of Nigeria, Gateway Bank and Global Bank, so were some other companies which were liquidated while because they consumed the resources of their stakeholders.

As I studied Ceno Ventures Ltd, I had many questions arose in my mind. These questions included "What keeps successful entrepreneurs moving?", "How far would an entrepreneur need to focus? and so on.

Without focus, it will be difficult to keep moving. Ceno Ventures Ltd disembodied from its merger in the year 2004 when it became necessary to keep moving. While the Chief Executive Officer, Mr. Ekeh Christian O, returned from his 6th business trip, two difficulties stood on his way. These difficulties were so disastrous that he lost his business capital when his goods were impounded by Nigeria Customs Service following the ban on used compressors (H.S. Code 8414.3000), used air conditioners (H.S. Codes 8415.1000.11 8415.9000.99) and used fridges / freezers (H.S. Codes 8418.1000.11 8418.6900), and the company had no money to begin with. Ceno Ventures Ltd, I shall raise a missile against failure in your name. It was an adversary similar to most companies, including Innoson Group Nigeria Ltd in 2004/2005, when his twenty-five containers of CKD parts were held at seaport by Nigeria Customs Service.

The answer which I discovered that keeps every

entrepreneur moving despite all oppositions is valuable. It has a price, though the price cannot match its value. You may have found it in chapter four. The answer is possessed by Ceno Ventures Ltd, Innoson Group Nigeria Ltd and so many other successful entrepreneurs. This answer is the number seven of the ***Basic Principles of Success*** and ***Law-15 of Enduring Success***. Without it, it is difficult for one to achieve and endure success.

Ceno Ventures Ltd did not get its chance as years went by. All of us who went through trials and tribulations knew that living fire begot cold and impotent ash at last. No downturn will last till the end of time. When the opportunity came again, it appeared in a different form. It was neither in the way Ceno had expected it. That is one funny thing about opportunity. It does not really come knocking, but when you move out to seize it, you may end up in more different accomplishments hence you listen and understand your inner audience. Most times, it appears in the form of misfortune, and impure mind won't recognize it.

Recently, Ceno Ventures Ltd recorded millions of fortune with an outstanding success prior to its merger. Out of Mr. Christian's business experiences, he had proved something more spectacular. He had proved that a quitter cannot get to the end, and that ending is everything (the ending is where the success will begin to manifest).

Law Eleven
Appeal To People's Self Interest

"On The Journey Of Successful Living, Most People Run, And They Get Tired. Others Lag, And They're Still Lagging. I Jog, And I'm Still Jogging. The Journey Has No End At Last" - **Ekeh Joe Obinna**

Appeal to people's self interest by cultivating the '***power of reassurance***' whenever you have succeeded in making them pay attention to you, your products or services. Lure them with irresistible gains, services or products. It feels good to sow courtesy and kindness because you'll reap a good friendship and gather all love. In the business community, real power and success are attained through good friendship. The patterns of good friendship and the capacities to form them are undoubtedly more important than fame, popularity, function, role or high positions.

The majority of people who fail to acquire wealth sufficiently are mostly generally the people who have also failed to sustain sufficient attention of others. They are influenced by the counsel of others that a particular territory, race, city or state is not necessary or needed. Anyone should depend upon this *law*. It leads to attracting **love** from one another. One may earn fortunes in return for minimum amount of labour and applied effort but this does not happen without a simple application of this particular **law**. It ensures every person the opportunity to be depended upon in order to render useful services or products, and also the opportunity to receive blessings in the form of money, reputation, fame and riches in proportion to the value of the services.

This principle known as the **law of love** is a force no man can beat. Check the **law** well. It is in unification with all the known basic principles of living success mentioned in chapter four of this book. When you have people's interest at heart, you will not love to give them inferior products or services, and they will love you. And when they love you, they will depend on you, your products or your services. At the end, there will be success.

"If you need to turn to an ally for help, do not bother to remind him of your past assistance and good deeds. He

will find a way to ignore you. Instead, uncover something in your request, or in your alliance with him, that will benefit him, and emphasise it out of all proportion. He will respond enthusiastically when he sees something to gain for himself." - Robert Greene.

Law Twelve
Stand Out

"Conform Not Yourselves To The Standard Of This World" - **Holy Bible**

We're all prone to developments in business communities, and dealing with them both the positive and the negative changes is as much about recognizing the changes from a psychological standpoint as it is about everyone adopting his own strategy. To help get enhancement on your performance, whether it is your job performance or performance of your product in the marketplace, I have come with the knowledge that the best orientation you can adopt when pursuing your goals, improving your market performance, or when introducing your products to market community is neither to depend on general strategies. The best advice is to adopt '***Outstanding***' Strategies. Most individuals and business initiators put more attention on what is working, instead of focusing on problems and perceived weaknesses. This is also the rule of outstanding business success. Everyone may be known to one particular strategy, but be conspicuous at all cost.

Who wants what is normal and what is common or unattractive? Nobody will buy your products if they don't notice who you are or what they are. Everything is judged by appearance. Things of lesser notice catch lesser attention. Put yourself forward to get your business on the map. All the successful men and companies I have investigated never let their businesses, products or services get lost in the crowd- they're Outstanding.

The majority of people may be limited to a certain level of business success. Others may be lagging, but outstanding successful people have just one thing in common. They don't just sit or stand with the crowd. They simply have an absolute sense of mission. No matter how valuable you and your ideas are, humanity will certainly attempt to play both of you down. So exclude yourself from their standpoint. When they court you in, court them out; when they court you out, court them in.

If it is service you render, carve out few clients or industries and become their most dominant consultant. Don't fight with narrow minded people who are also competing with your products or services. Be determined to compel them to change their mindsets about who you stand to be, not by imitating or manipulating their services or products but by focusing on what you do every day. If they change it, fine; if they don't, fine. The good news is that you are pursuing excellence.

Law Thirteen
No Idle Fund

"A Rich Man Is Nothing But A Poor Man With Money."
- **W.C. Fields**

This law is often a necessity for paid workers. Keeping idle funds is never a dependable way of accumulating riches and acquiring wealth. One's financial health and success depends upon one's respect for, and application of this law. Successful business people understand this law. They follow the advice of financial experts which is against keeping too much cash idle in order to get the maximum rate of return on their investments

These idle funds are simply funds that are not deposited in an interest bearing or investment tracking machines. All funds that is not participating in the economic markets of your business ventures. These funds are often thought of as "*idle funds*" since they do not appreciate in any manner. These may not be funds that have appreciated in your retirement account (as an individual), but you may want to consider funds in your savings account. There is one option which individuals may earn income on idle funds while maintaining liquidity of those funds and that is to invest in financial market or short-term interest accounts that will provide the depositor with a short-term rate of interest. Funds don't make funds when you make them idle funds. The richer you are the richer you should be. This explains why the rich gets richer.

Most financial institutions such as Access Bank Plc, First Bank Plc, Zenith Bank Plc, Fidelity Bank Plc, Stanbic Bank Plc and Diamond Bank Plc, speaking after a complete analysis, will grant you a sizeable interest rate on Treasure Bill, Fixed Deposit, Shares, Bond or Mutual Funds, and so on.

If it is riches you seek. Never neglect this **law**. However, it is as good as violating the third law of enduring success outlined herein. No intelligent person will either request or expect financial empowerment without investing a seed of an equivalent.

Law Fourteen
Avoid The Pessimist

"Optimists Are Right. So Are Pessimists. It's Up To You To Choose Which One You Want To Be With." - **Harvey Mackay**

A generous and noble spirit cannot be expected to dwell in the breasts of men who are pessimistic in the journey of success, hoping for, and beyond their daily bread. The more you get closer to them, the more they will try to influence your thinking orientation. To seek advice from a pessimist will be fatal, as well as trying to please him. "I don't know the key to success, but the key to failure is trying to please everybody." - Bill Cosby.

Upon observation of this law, the two pieces of news I brought to you is simple. A very good news and a very bad one. I will start with the bad news. Everything you constantly think in your mind becomes reality. Accept it. It's the philosophy of nature and humanity. You should know the very truth between the blessings of God and faith, the very philosophical chemistry which only but few men know and understand; and yet, many who do not know about it boast of it. If you think everything will go wrong, at some point, things will go wrong. If you think relationship is difficult, you will have a difficult time running a relationship, if you think you won't succeed, you will fail. And when you make a habit out of pessimism, your whole life will begin to break down in pieces with every thought you think, and you'll become a difficult person and pretty stressful among others. This is the bad news.

This element, mood, is contagious and infectious as a virus disease. Especially in the workplace where many people spend about ten hours or more with co-workers. One negative-pessimistic attitude can spread around the workplace, resulting in poor communication with co-workers and inducing stress by complaining, being hurtful, impatient and careless. It can also reduce productivity and can cause distractions.

But, avoid them. They will not harm you or affect your job performance if you do not sympathize them- that is the good news. You may feel you are helping a drowning man but you are only uprooting your own success to plant the seed of an extraordinary failure generated by another person. The pessimist sometimes (and he often does) draws misfortune on himself. He will also draw it on you. Associate with the optimist and fortunate instead. They are omnipotent now and always.

Every person whose mind is already purified must endeavour to make certain that he chooses the right team to work with. Only by so doing can he be sure of maintaining the state of mind immune to negative thinking. The standard at which you choose your friends or co-workers today and relieve the irrelevant ones, will define the elements which you are constantly exposed to. It is not sufficient to live in banks of water and wash your hand with spittle. Get rid of people who do not build you positively. Take advantage of one quiet hour or two in the early morning or at night and go to some solitary place where you know you will be absolutely free of distraction, and, having seated your mind in an easy attitude right away from the object of sentiments, in a calm and understanding spirit, check things very well and relieve people who you are not on the same page of thinking orientation with, and yet tend to cause you to change direction.

Law Fifteen
Do It For Love: If You Do Not Enjoy It, Don't Do It

"The Best Way To Predict Your Future Is By Understanding Your Inner Man Which Enables You To Handle Your Present." - **Ekeh Joe Obinna**

If you had to identify, in a simply study, the reason why man has not achieved, and cannot achieve his desire in fullness, even with all his academic qualifications and skills potentials, it may be because he's not doing what he wishes to do, he's doing what people wish him to do.

But, doing what you love is the cornerstone of having abundance in life. Man was not created to find a list of careers or desires he will choose from. He was created with freedom to generate his own career or desire. This generation of desire begins immediately at birth as man is born with emptiness of mind, yet during growth and development, certain emotions, traits, feelings, and other elements emerge. These elements will make up a **desire** for man based on what man has heard, seen, listened to, felt which simply determines the kinds of elements in his mind. The function of this formless continuum (mind) is to perceive, receive, accept, or reshape objects. And the product of mind is also formless and flexible. And it can also, within a short period of time, begin to change depending upon the objects it constantly receives.

Man may make his plans, choose a career or business, but the mind directs his actions. The mind of man speaks with divine authority; his decisions are always right. His way to successful living cannot get complicated if he follows his inner audience.

All the elements that make up the mind of man will create a specific desire for him. It will be different from other person's own. This does not mean that there won't be similarities with some other person(s). It simply expresses why man says "I can" and other person may say "he can't". Should man love his career, seldom does he feel disconnected from the challenges that first engaged his interest. He won't be influenced or simply care about what people think or say about him doing it. I don't mean this observation to sound self-centred, but the truth is that people who genuinely love their career don't allow others to talk them out of it. Any element that goes into the mind of man has results, but if man loves his career, every element has positive influence for him.

Note: The state of the mind (the condition of the inner man) such as anger, jealousy, envy and disastrous attachment are all nothing but delusions. And these are the principal causes of all suffering. Man may think that his suffering is caused by other people, by poor material condition(s) or by society, but in reality it all comes from his own deluded state of mind. The essence of spiritual practice is to reduce and eventually eradicate altogether man's delusions, and to replace them with permanent inner peace. This is the real task of churches and mosques, and somehow, institutions of learning; to teach the real meaning of human life.

Law Sixteen
Forget The Price: Consider Superiority

The problem most unsuccessful companies and individuals encountered was because those who guided them underestimated the power of superiority. Their strategies and management advices became unreliable and impractical. Lessons from companies whose outstanding results may be considered more than corporate achievements revealed that it is better to be superior than to be cheaper. It is no other expression other than that similar to LAW-12. This rule is the foundational concepts on which companies and certain individuals whom I have statistically studied build their fame and financial empire. It also revealed that most companies barely made outstanding achievement(s) as a result of nothing but random fluctuations. In my study, I discovered something startling. If you decide to carry out this instruction or implement this law, the extent to which you implement it will determine clearly, how much or how little you love the people who may be interested in your end products or services, and how much you have extended in practice, to implement *law-11*. All successful companies and their diverse choices are certainly as great as obeying this elementary Law. Liquid capital, skills, brands and all other resources are good but they simply do not guarantee success.

How did these companies' leaders and successful

individuals come to adopt this law? I neither have any idea. Nor do I know whether the executives of these companies or the individuals even follow the law consciously. But I discovered that fortunes gravitate to the companies or individuals whose minds are prepared to simply obey this law. In other words, they compete on differentiation other than price. That is, they prioritise increasing quality to affect revenue over reducing costs and standard.

While Intercontinental Bank Plc was among the largest financial institution as regards financial services providers in West Africa. As of December 2008, the bank's shareholders equity was valued at approximately 1.7 billion US dollar (NGN: 261 billion). This financial institution acquired controlling shareholding in Equity Bank of Nigeria, and became a commercial bank in 1996. That same year, it also acquired majority shareholding in West African Provincial Company Plc. (WAPIC), an insurance company.

In the year 2005, Intercontinental Bank Plc reached a greater higher station, to be successfully merged with more three other commercial banks, in which it held equity positions prior to the merger; namely Equity Bank of Nigeria, Gateway Bank and Global Bank.

I have neither seen anyone who obeyed the principles of prosperity and remained the same. Nor have I known anyone who distinguishes himself, without expression of contempt, but with love for the people who may be interested in his end product and remained lagging in business. The truth is that every failure is as a result of complication(s) coming from violated laws, most times unknown. When Intercontinental Bank Plc became under-capitalized and troubled, it was not that the commercial bank had not been properly staffed to be immune to failure or environmental challenges. It was not that it had not been applying sufficient business intelligence known to it. Yet, the bank consumed the resources of its stakeholders despite all management advices and maintenance. It joined about other 139 financial institutions which had gone underground, leaving only 25 banks in Nigeria.

The truth is that people who freely practice Law-15 do not always know when they implement Law-16, and same goes to others. That's why you should understand that these laws are interrelated. It's a carefully joint commandment to achieve and endure success.

Law Seventeen
Lead And Harmonize In Your Host Community

Business communities have certainly changed, and they require new conventional strategies. The uncertain economic outlook and the relentless pace of technological advances make today's entrepreneurial adventure much more challenging for today's young entrepreneurs. This means that successful companies must defend their positions because their products can go out of fashion just as quickly as they do not expect it.

Group Managing Director of Access Bank Plc, Mr. Aigboje Aig-Imokhuede understands this law. After so many banks subsided, he learnt more about concept of sustainability, to put companies in harmony with their host community. When he talked about host community, he actually meant the community where you operate. If you are in Edo State, Lagos State, or Federal Capital Territory-Abuja, that is your host community. If you operate across Nigeria, that is your host community, and if you operate across the whole world, the entire globe is your host community. Those that maintain that harmony are the companies that survive yearly. They may change name, management, and shareholding, yet they are able to achieve their end goals and stand out.

In 2009, a special audit of the commercial banks in Nigeria by the Central Bank of Nigeria, the country's banking regulator, found nine of Nigerian banks to be under-capitalized and badly managed. Intercontinental Bank Plc was one of the troubled banks. Following the injection of capital by the federal government of Nigeria, to maintain solvency, the troubled banks had embarked on re-capitalization through participation by new investors.

In the year 2011, Access Bank Plc expressed its earnest interest to keep moving to a higher station. It was evident enough that its business achievement had turned down the offer of setback and failure. When Access Bank Plc began talks with the Central Bank of Nigeria to acquire Intercontinental Bank Plc, Access Bank Plc had pursued significant capital increase throughout the remaining year of 2005. I'm not unmindful that the bank had suffered internal challenges which other banks may have also experienced. But I have neither known anyone who obeys Law-4 outlined herein and seems not to be prepared for downturn as well as being immune to major setback and failure.

When this *desire* to acquire a fellow financial institution reached the position for approval, the shareholders of Intercontinental Bank Plc and Access Bank Plc, the Federal High Court of Nigeria, the Central Bank of Nigeria, the Securities and Exchange Commission, made the approval that same year of 2005. Access Bank Plc and Intercontinental Bank Plc announced the completion of the recapitalization of Intercontinental Bank Plc and the acquisition of 75% majority interest in Intercontinental Bank Plc by Access Bank Plc. From that day forward, Intercontinental Bank Plc, including all its assets, liabilities and undertakings, became a subsidiary of

Access Bank Plc. Access Bank Plc then ended its pursue for capital increase in the year 2007. The bank simply achieved this while implementing Law-15 and Law-17, because they also tried to prioritize Law-4, Law-11 and Law-16 in their business.

Law Eighteen
Do Not Buy Things You Do Not Need
"A Fool And His Money Is One Big Party." -

"I have enough money to last me the rest of my life unless I buy something." - Jackie Mason. Ten out of hundred of today's graduates are guilty of violating this particular law. This is because of the manner of which they were programmed by school system(s) to find a paid job, they were not prepared to understand the effect of financial promiscuity; to be financially prepared to keep moving when job opportunity didn't come so fast. Hence **they buy things they don't really need to impress people they don't really know, with money they barely earn.** Long before I graduated, till today, people still practice this style. They have accumulated to the number of unemployed youths owing to possible debts they have accumulated which now hinder them from keeping up. They think they will begin paying back once they gain employment. This is worse than a virus affliction of Ebola. If you are a man or a woman undertaking a journey to achieve your financial freedom as a first time employee, do not buy things you don't need if your financial freedom is really important to you. You are cautioned to be reasonable with your spending. This law is in harmony with Law-9 and Law-10 expressed herein, under the **Basic Law of Enduring Success** followed by every successful men and women who have accumulated great fortunes to the height they may have desired.

In a mechanical engineering workshop, the rule is "safety first." Capital is the number one thing every new and old business idea needs to keep up. Save every fund you can because you can never know when you may need it. This may mean that you will have to pay your employees just as necessary than they want, or bargain down your supplier's prices even if your supplier is your best friend or a family member.

Law Nineteen
Invest No Borrowed Funds

"When Setback Comes, Loan Payment Does Not Fade Away." - **Ekeh Joe Obinna**

That you have successfully started a business is not a guarantee that you will succeed at once. Many business owners cover their start-up costs entirely through loans, with the expectation that they will begin paying back the loans with the profits from their new business. New businesses may take months or years to generate significant profit(s). However, loan payments can really become a millstone around the neck of any business initiator. If you borrow money, you may be exposing your new business idea to a fairly large business expense. You may have to make loan payments when your new business idea requires a greater financial support. This usually happen during a business's start-up or an expansion. And if you have problems paying back the loan or keeping up with the payments due to possible setback, you may ruin your passion for your business idea. Loan(s) sought from commercial lenders may also require you to pledge property as security for the loan, and if you don't repay the loan, the lender may take the property and sell it to recoup the money. If you pledge business property as security for the loan, and your business slows down or meets setback that you cannot meet with the loan payments as agreed, you may lose those valuable assets just when you need them the most. Worse, if you pledge personal assets, such as your house or stock portfolio, you risk losing them to pay a business debt. Even if you organize your business as a corporation or a limited liability company (each of which provides owners with limited liability for business debts), almost all commercial lenders will require you, as the owner of a new or small business, to personally guarantee the loan, or to pledge personal assets to cover the loan, which wipes out this limited liability.

But this *law* does not suggest you should not seek loan to simply improve your end product(s). It simply expresses the fact that loan does not truly come with guarantee if the operator is a first-timer. Because, ***when setback comes, loan payment does not fade away.*** Loan may best benefit those who are already on the journey, far beyond starting, or those who have acquired sufficient assets to liquidate in place of the loan without going a long way down.

If you can save up as much of the start-up capital yourself before you open your doors, you will help ensure that loans won't sink your new business idea. Remember, also, that there is an outside chance that a lender may add unfavourable terms that can sink your little profit(s) if your business isn't as successful as you initially planned. If you provide as much of the start-up capital as possible, it will lessen the odds of nasty surprises hindering your mind to remain calm towards your business idea. However, if your new business idea is limited by capital, it may best benefit you if you invite friends and family members who share the same vision as you do, to invest in your business and become part owners, instead of simply lending you funds. Such investors often have same business passion and can offer you valuable advice, moral support, and professional assistance.

Note: Loan only gives you time to start or initiate your business without waiting for too long to realize the total required business capital. This means that any business debtor should have a solid plan or sufficient money to pay his lender even if the success of his business idea delays or does not come at all.

Law Twenty
Recognition And Appreciation Is Everything

"*I Am Not Afraid Of Failure, I Know It Does Not Occur Where There's True Love And Appreciation.*"- **Ekeh Joe Obinna**

In the middle of composing my research report of successful companies and business initiators, a terrible realization came over me. I began to wonder, ***does people know that many will suffer loss owing to possible lack of appreciation?***

In the course of this, you will soon find out the enemy that is standing between you and noticeable achievements. You will find out not only why you have failed to recognize opportunities, but also why your subconscious mind have failed to exhibit the basic principles of success which was meant to be supreme right from birth. This power of appreciation is the one of the most undcrused force in today's business communities.

The story is known in history, in Nigeria, about a struggle of an institution of higher learning named Institute of Management and Technology (IMT) Enugu, whose aim was to educate and train successful business initiators and employers of labour. It came into existence in the city of Enugu, in the year 1973 and had been in operation to educate the hearts, the minds and the brains of men and women. But the required educational system came and faded away, and did not come back quickly. For many years, it remained a lagging institution of higher learning. Countless people came and went with more or little education. Students spent their prime resources trying to learn in an un-conducive training perimeter. It was this same expression of **lack of appreciation** that brought about over population of qualified and not qualified large number of students whose interests were only to acquire certificates. On 30th September, 2011, the National Board for Technical Education withdrew accreditation for all courses offered by the institution. This is an institution of higher learning which had plenty of tangible evidence for success and worldly recognition, but it lost out because its management were self-seeking instead of thinking of their end products (students). The going was very hard for the dedicated students. People who came across the graduates of the institution understood complete poor products. In 2012, a new leadership came. The lesson had been well learnt. A new management system came to place which mandated the institution to **recognize** their first role and value, not only their students, but also their host community. It was indeed a major shift based on experiences and sincere observations of having violated Law-3, Law-4, and Law-11.

From that time on, the institution did not only apply Law-17, it also prioritised Law-12 and Law-16. Students now learn so fast, and very freely. New structures were made.

The secret of attaining success is inseparably attached to the Power of recognition and appreciation. ***Failure does not occur where there is supreme power of appreciation***. Today, Institute of Management and Technology (IMT) Enugu does not only educate the hearts of men and women to have good men and women, but it also educates the brains and the minds to have good skilful men and women that can use their minds to attract riches and wealth without passing bad feelings to society. If one wants to talk about such men and women, one should be guided in calmness, to a thousand of men and women whose forces of thought are re-united and whose minds are ever prepared for the highest level of wealth and riches in financial market, in movie/music industry, and in all other world of creativity, in true sincere faith. Ekeh Joe Obinna is one of them.

Law Twenty-one
Be Passionate About Effective Communication

"Correct Me If I'm Wrong, But Hasn't The Fine Line Between Employed Youths And Unemployed Youths Gotten Finer? Today, He Who Loses Communication Intelligence Loses Much." - **Ekeh Joe Obinna**

Civilization has changed the way we interact as humans. As a direct result of this transition, more graduates are entering the workforce with malformed sets of social skills. Upon the understanding of the need for living success and financial freedom, it's your job to go into self-education and teach yourself skills that only but successful people possess. These are the percentage of people who go through the tunnel with their lamps in their bags so that when they get to the end of the tunnel and there is no light, they will put on their lamps. They must not wait for job opportunity. Their lamps are on their lamp-stands for others to see. Bukky Bello will tell a volume about this.

Communication is not an important thing, it's everything important in business community. With global business transactions continually increasing, the need for effective communication to meet global demand is also increasing. If you find out you're weak in communication, you are sure you're not being pessimistic, or you do not hate people who are interested in your end product(s), centre your attention on this instruction.

Bear it in mind that listening is not the same as hearing. Learn to listen not only to the words being spoken, but how they are being spoken and the non-verbal messages that are sent with them. Use the techniques of clarification and reflection to confirm what the other person has said and avoid any confusion. Try not to think about what to say next whilst listening; instead clear your mind and focus on the message being received. Try not to be judgemental or biased by preconceived ideas or beliefs; instead view situations and responses from the other person's perspective, staying securely in tune with your own emotions which will enable you to understand the emotions of others. ***Any one who loses this communication intelligence loses much***. Your clients, customers or partners will appreciate effective communication when you make them feel welcomed, wanted, valued or appreciated in your communications. If you let others know that they are valued, they are much more likely to give you their best. And you will know what is coming next to you when you have effectively listened to your clients and observed all the non-verbal messages. You will not be able to look into the future while on the journey of successful living without communication intelligence, because most times, you need to look and understand. Your client may say something while his non-verbal words may express a different thing that only a good communicator can understand.

Success in many walks of life is attributed to effective communication. The differences in culture, religion or race may require you to understand the terms commonly used in your immediate environment that other culture(s), religion, race or environment may find offensive.

There is no substitute for effective communication in every business community. It cannot be supplanted by many other technical and social skills. Those who have effective communication skills seem to enjoy immunity during economic meltdown. No matter how drastic a meltdown may appear, they seem to be prepared for it.

Law Twenty-two
Embrace The Fear Of Sex

"Life Is One Big Party When You Are Still Young."

Sex, what a powerful tool! It is pleasing to human vanity to believe that sex is fun. But not until man begins to report to himself, in sincerity of truth and upon purified mind, the true condition in which he discovers himself as a result of his indulgence in the act of sex. This setback of sex is not an abstract something outside man. It is an experience which the majority of young men and women find themselves indulging in. The sad truth about man is that he cannot be reborn. Until man identifies the causes of his setback and suffering, he is ineligible for freedom and prosperity; and most men are self-inflicted. Owing to possible spiritual emptiness and ignorance, man cannot identify the causes of his physical suffering which is as a result of complicated spirit. This complication results from spiritual unification which rigidly happens during sexual intercourse, because this act of sex occurs with a wrong partner in most instances.

Nature made it quite plainly that "***two will become one***", for they have joined their souls with one another. Embrace the fear of this ***spiritual unification*** if the freedom and happiness of your inner man is important to you. The fact is that man has endured in the belief that is rooted in ignorance of the true nature of the influence of the subject matter. Understand that man must be prepared to accept that the places which he exposed himself to, knowledge which he sought for, element which he brought into his soul, has made him.

Should institutions of learning, churches, mosques, NGOs, organizational leaders, including households, organize a continuous lecture on the subject matter of '***sex***' and '***spirituality?***'

Sex is biological but it has influence to the mental, physical, and spiritual states of man. Any man who encourages his indulgence in the act of sex tends to carry out a complete spiritual unification with his partner. Nature made it so. Ignorance of this knowledge is capable of causing men, as well as women, their privilege to simple access to happiness, wealth, and riches; and hence draws the dark shadows of sorrow, pain, misfortune, failure, and so on, to settle upon their souls.

While on the journey of successful living, between the ages of forty and fifty-five, which is the most productive period of life, is when most men begin to realize that they stumble along with weary and uncertain steps, that they seem to be bound to struggling with unrealistic desire which comes from nowhere, and has no certain gain. This realization unavoidably falls upon men, as well as women, who retraced their steps to recheck. Caryn Leschen, a freelance illustrator and copywriter observed this when she says that "Thirty-five is when you finally get your head together and your ***body*** starts falling apart." Then the true knowledge of sex generally manifests to man unavoidably. Until then, man begins to understand the true mystery and spiritual effects of sexual intercourse on him by earnest self examinations. Man does not strive to realize this knowledge, it will freely fall upon him because it is more than a mere theory that the emotion of sex is a passing phase. It is only a self created negative shadow that reflects and transfers, from a partner, all the elements of consequences which he or she is suffering from, for having disobeyed the law of his or her own being.

On the journey of successful living, man may rise and fall as consequences of his indulgence in the act with a wrong person (bad blood). He may experience an infinite struggling for financial freedom and living success as a result of his covenant with unknown laws (a transferred spirit). He automatically brings into his being a new spirit through the act of sex. The understanding and the teaching of this subject of sex is, today, undermined by churches, institutions of learning, households, and so on. Understand that having sex can be as fateful as doing drugs. Both can change the state of the mind and reduce focus. They can bring into being, a weak mind (complicated spirit). They can lead to bondage with unknown *laws* to a very long time in life.

All of man's problem- misfortune, diseases and sicknesses, poverty, spinsterhood, stealing, anger, hatred, greed, failure, self-affliction, and so on, come to him as a result of *violated laws* owing to spiritual emptiness. These violations will result in a complicated spirit (impure mind), and it's transferable to the next man through gene, which happens during sexual intercourse. We all know people who begin to look alike when they started dating. We all know people who are easily influenced by their wives or husbands than any other person(s). This spiritual unification will make up man's inner audience and reshape his condition. Now, accept that this mind (inner man) does not attract to man what he wants, but he attracts to man what he (inner man) truly is. A complicated mind (impure mind) can only attract, desire, and achieve a complicated goal (impurities of life). This statement simply expresses that man is manacled only by himself. By first knowing, understanding, and obeying the laws of his being, man is made stronger.

This law of '***embracing the fear of sex***' was not created by I, Ekeh Joe Obinna. It has been there all along. The wall(s) which man builds around himself through his indulgence in the act is all nothing but illusion. No man (spiritual being) is actually created, in reality, to look pleasant and attractive in his natural clothes. Be man in sincere mind, there is no truth in the statement that man cannot sleep in a single bed with an opposite sex without being attracted to the opposite sex. The truth is that, man has first conceived the thought, in the frame of his mind, he has used his imagining faculty to reflect what he had seen, heard, done, or images he stored in his mind. His continuous indulgence in the act is as a result of spiritual unification - a covenant (a new law) which he has automatically created for himself by his mere indulgence in the act. Man with sufficient willpower and intelligence can discourage the presence of any emotion of sex within him. Nature has provided man with the chemistry of the mind which permits man to, knowingly or unknowingly, make choices of laws with spirit beings. These covenants (these laws) will continue to multiply faster as man changes sex partner.

Seldom does man accept that there is no failure that is not as a result of ignorance and violation of unknown laws and principles, and which will not, if man is ready to learn its lesson, take man to success and vanish away. These unknown laws are made known above. There are advices and guidelines in the next chapter of this book. The presence of these **laws** in any man defines a self-control, a knowledgeable, an intelligent, and a conquered mind. There are no other laws other than "***The Twenty-Two Laws of Enduring Success***". So, change anything you must to follow all the laws to the end. These simple laws neither dictate specific behaviour, nor are they even general strategies. If it does not work for you, the reason may be owing to the nature of your mind. Yet, these laws are the foundational mandate for which wealth and riches are attained and also may be endured. You may carry within you some certain traits of character which may hold your faith and belief against these laws or some of them. But they are interrelated. So you should not conceive the thought of adopting only few, to neglect others.

These laws state that all situations around you is all about how, what, and who you are. It also attracts to you, not just one thing but many things at once. The natural observation is that all the obstacles you meet on your way are part of the whole black picture- influences from made and unmade laws, which is your background. For this reason, these laws can't be used as a general strategy owing to differences in thinking orientation, even though it would be wonderful if it could. It will work for you because it has worked for the majority of men and women. So you may want to go back to re-read these **laws** after you have completed the whole manual.

Seven

LETTER TO GOVERNMENT LEADERS, SECURITIES, YOUTHS, AND PARENTS

In 2001, National Population Commission recorded that youths under the age of 30 constitute half of the approximately 150 million unemployed Nigerians. Research analysis and statement by Doreo Partners in 2013 also stated that unemployment rate in Nigeria was growing at the rate of 16% per year with the youth impacting the most, and accounting for three times the general unemployment.

? Letter To Government

Leaders, there is a point at which everything becomes simply disturbing and there is no longer any question of choice, because all you have staked will be lost if you look back. Life is a journey of no return. There is truth in the statement that you do not inherit the nation from your predecessors, you borrowed it from the youths. Government organized and conducted only for self-interest individuals or groups give birth to poverty and a short lifespan to society. It brings all about hatred and damages the survival of every one in the land. It's also a display of disrespect and lack of self-worth. In history, in society, there were people who sweated, fought and bled for the country. The death of these great and noble men who sought that this country could emerge and survive should not be in vain. I raise my voice in caution to all opinion leaders, opposition to government usually just bring about violence. It is a great attack to the streets, and to society at large. It is possible we can bring about an eventual reform by simply withdrawing from any dangerous cooperation. People have expressed dissatisfactory and disagreement in silence by simply not cooperating with government leaders again. And in history, such have brought the death of so many noble men and good citizens, death of a government and society at large. "What do I owe to my time, to my country, to my neighbours, to my friends? Such are the questions which a virtuous man ought often to ask himself." - Lavater.

On the other hand, it is obvious that government may be working hard for all the people but without the support of all people. What the people of the country want is very simple. They want a Nigeria as good as its promises. Now, the people have also failed to understand that ***government of a country*** cannot cry, laugh, or smile, it is just an organized idea of every individual who is alive, in society, have. It cannot bleed. Everybody who organizes his abilities and labour to the call of civilization is '***the government***. Good roads, stable power supply, potable drinking water, clean environment, good and quality schools, all these do not spring up from the air and start working automatically for everybody's benefits. They come in response to the ideas expressed, efforts emitted, time emitted, love shared, organized labour of some men and women in society. These are men and women who have good imagination, sincere faith, hope, pure desire, passion and love, good choices for their lives and that of the country, so as to improve in civilization. These men and women are 'THE GOVERNMENT'.

I write to you, all opinion leaders, because you have known it from the beginning that school leavers have increased and unemployment cannot be completely resolved. Youths with sincere heart and good faith are disappointed as they cannot overcome the wilderness of unemployment on their own. We must not keep doing the new thing the old way. We must not be afraid to go too far to support our youths. We must not be afraid to combine or introduce **financial education** and **principles of living success** to our youths in institutions of higher learning, and during the National Youth Service orientation course, because particles of living success lie beyond formal education. The fine thick line between successful graduates and failures has also gotten finer owing to many factors, including inadequate financial skills among them.

Government, we can have a glorious future soon. Most youths have decided to go into becoming employers of labour and entrepreneurs. We can support them and we must support them. They are equally strategic and as well precious to the nation's economy. It is a great privilege to have youths who are job opportune and those who own businesses in the land. It is also literally true that government of a society can succeed most when they help youths in the land succeed in one business endeavour or the other. Every country benefits from a society of ambitious overachievers who never stopped wondering how to **keep moving**.

Sometimes my thoughts and worries do not let me fall asleep, and even when I finally fall asleep, I do not sleep soundly. I do not have fear, I do not have negative thoughts because, I only see improvement each time I have unsound sleep owing to deep thoughts and worries. Dear government, insecurity can be improved. Here is a realistic suggestion.

? *Letter To The Security Department(s)*

Unemployment may have been a global crisis which simply needs a global attention, and also have been the reasons behind the increment in crime rate in the land, because many are unemployed. Hence people of every society commit crime and get away with it, they tend to leave room for more crime, and influencing others to join in crime life seems easier. But our security can be enhanced. Unemployment can be sizeably reduced. When security is downgraded, people may find it easier to induce others into crime, as they settle for less without pushing their true potentials.

I write to you, all security departments, insecurity has contributed about 47.8 percent to increasing crime rate in the land; and have in one way enhanced unemployment by 19.3 percent. As people of society, most especially youths, have preferred to risk their lives in illegal businesses instead of put their resources in legal business ideas and opportunities. But security can be improved by sixty percent, if not more. I propose to you, police department(s) and other relative security department(s) to collaborate to design a Digital National Security Online Database in which will bear the details of every citizen who has acquired his/her national identity card from federal government, through the services of National Identity Management Commission (NIMC). A citizen who is eighteen year old has reached the stage of choice making. This means that such a citizen has become, and can assume responsibilities for his actions and inactions. Let Nigerian Immigration Service Commission remember what it is, National Identity Management Commission (NIMC) too, and make it mandatory for every citizen who is eighteen years and above to secure his/her national identity card which has come with a tracking number. And this tracking number should be assigned to the National Security Online Database which will be managed by security departments. This simply means that each citizen will have a profile-account in the National Security Online Database where he/she can update any of his/her legal properties such as cars, lands, houses, and so on. This means that when a citizen buys a car and updates it to his National Security Database and it goes missing, the police can easily look up to see who buys the car next. That way, lands, houses, hand phones, cars and all other things that come with serial number, which the owner has updated to his/her National Security Account cannot be illegally sold. Once police stops a citizen and investigates the serial number, vehicle particulars, land particulars, and so on, and your particulars are not updated to any national security account, bearing the citizen's identity tracking number, the citizen automatically becomes a suspect. This also means that once a citizen is caught in crime(s), the police would investigate him/her, and upon found guilty of the crime in the law court, the authorities would update his/her account with the report of the crime he or she committed. That way, when a company needs to hire one's service, or wants to employ one, they will only have to request his/her security transcript assigned to his/her tracking number directly from security departments. This means that security services in embassy can be enhanced, illegal immigrates could be controlled. Militants and terrorists would be reduced and downgraded. This also means that employees and employers who still think that one can accumulate riches by bribery and corruption, or mere organizing of payroll of workers under their jurisdictions to deduct monies from their salaries and wages, or those who prepare names of ghost workers to embezzle monies and other benefits from government, would have a greater risk to face as every government worker would have his/her national identity tracking number reviewed for clearance and payments.

Unemployment is a reproach. I never heard of poverty. The truth is that the idea of government may constitute only but a poor solution to the issue of unemployment and it's about 36.9% responsible for the fate faced by most school leavers. Insecurity, poor water supply, poor power supply, bribery and corruption, exam malpractices, impersonation, fraud, ghost working, including unsuccessful employees and unemployed youths are the causes of increment in the rate of unemployment. When any one of these environmental traits is downgraded, the other is resolved. Unemployment is not just the problem, failure is. I refuse to believe that people who were employed years ago, till date, have not achieved anything. They have not become successful and they cannot employ others who follow after them because they have not been putting investments together and have not considered they should retire within 55 and 60 years of age. It is expected that a company employs you and in time to come you employ others, as much as you can. But they can't because they have not been following their dreams. Most of them are afraid of environmental traits. They had accepted the roles society foisted on them. Till date, they are struggling with financial issues. Yet they blame their plights on friends, parents, or governments.

During the hand-over ceremony of the Abuja Electricity Distribution Company to its new owner, Kann Utility Consortium Nigeria Limited, the Minister of Power, Prof. Chinedu Nebo, stated that government had paid out the sum of N360 billion naira only to disengaged workers of the defunct PHCN (The Punch 5th May, 2014) that was all they got and maybe look forward to being employed again, most of them would go into one business or the other. This was the job that made most of them to submit their personal ambition and the freedom to live their own life in their own way at earlier stage of life.

Youth unemployment has created "*a generation at risk*" stated by International Labour Organization. A strategic report analysis on the issue revealed that the worldwide youth unemployment will rise to 12.8 percent by 2018.

In the developed economies, the youth unemployment rate - unemployment among those aged 16 to 24- is approximately 18.1 percent. While the rate of Germany stands at 9 percent, those of the UK and the U.S. are 20 percent and 16 percent respectively, while in Spain and Greece half of the young people are jobless."- CNBC.

It is the idea(s) of society that will downgrade most of these environmental traits, if not all. That idea(s) of the people is called GOVERNMENT. It is not just a particular group that will decide your fate. There is a man every man is destined to become. Don't be stopped by thoughts of your own mind.

In my mind, the only time I have problem is when I sleep. Because that is the only time I stop thinking. Life is not a rehearsal. Youths, the only time you have is now, and your first commandant is something needs to happen. Nigeria is our country. If you have love for your race only then segregation and discrimination are what you demonstrate.

? Letter To Youths

Because my courage is fortified, I write to you, youths, for you may have known little. On journey of successful living and acquisition of wealth, everything is resolved into your own inward experience. If ever there is a future where we do not meet one on one, I would want you to know and always remember that you can become anyone you desire to be with more or little schooling. Every Nigerian is braver than he realizes, stronger than he knows, and greater than he thinks. But the most important thing I would want you to know is that government is not against you, the world is not against you, and your family members are proud of you.

We are a team. Life is good. It is better to hold a hand than to point a finger. I am here because you are there. But there are only few problems in life - health, money, food and relationship are all part of it. Make the right choice and you will live the right life.

It is obvious today that Nigeria has defaulted on this promissory call of reservation of humanity as her citizens of religions are concerned. Churches treat man like goat, mosques treat man like sheep but factions in religions have succeeded in changing the way goat and sheep should react to each other. Youths of various religious and different ethnic backgrounds have failed to honour the civil obligation, to uphold Nigeria's love and unity. We ask the nation not to think in terms of North and South, East and West, Muslims and Christians, but as Nigerians.

Let us not seek to satisfy our thirst for freedom by drinking from the cup of bitterness and hatred. There is no cause for pride in what has happened in our educational system, economy and security departments. There is no cause for self satisfaction in the long denial of equal rights of millions of Nigerians. But there is cause for hope and faith in being a youth. It is a great privilege to be young. Our mission is at once the oldest and the most basic of the nation, to draw up hope and strength. Be a good Nigerian. Obey the clarion call. We must forever conduct our struggle and quest for financial freedom on the high plane of dignity and discipline. If you can make it through ***school*** there is a brighter life. Nigeria is calm. It is our political parties that are not calm. Though Nigeria gave birth to political parties, political parties have given birth to Militants and Boko Haram.

There have been issues of war and peace, issues of terrorism and kidnapping, issues of prosperity and depression. But to the value of our dear youths and to the greatness of our great nation, there is no northern problem, there is no southern crisis, there is only one Nigeria facing little problem; and we, youths, can stick our strengths together to push it away.

Don't deny your brothers. Man is better than animal because he has kinsman. We're all distant relatives. We just spread out all over the whole nation as we adopt different religions and languages. Every man will be successful if he keeps moving on the right path. These are not just empty theories. In the name of Nigeria, these words are promises that every sincere heart shall share in the dignity of man. Never speak disrespectfully of your society. Only people who can't get into the nation will do that.

We must not wait months after months in the wilderness of unemployment. The only thing that comes to a sleeping man is dream, likewise the only thing that comes to an unemployed youth is crime. It is your choice that you do not settle for lesser than you're worth ***after schooling***. Don't be stopped by the thoughts of your own mind. Believe inside that you can't be beaten, believe that a common employable unemployed youth can develop from within and see himself rise to his highest station.

I write to you, youths, because riches and poverty are right in your hands. They are dwelling in your mind, in the constitution of your own thoughts. ***Keep Moving....***

When this book was in A4 format, I printed it as a handout note and shared it in a seminar titled **'Youth Empowerment'** organized by 'Co-Creators Universe, a non-governmental organization that is into wealth creation, poverty reduction, youth empowerment, and so on. It was barely sixty-eight pages of long note book. Few days later, somebody wrote to me saying "*Young man, I read your handout and it was great. I wish I read it in 2003. I would not have been struggling financially till today. I know it's now in the past, but what can I really do now? The education foundations I have laid for my children are poor. Should I become successful today it would still be of no use for I cannot go back to change the fact that I enrolled my children in poor oriented school owing to poor financial power. My son is in primary six and he had the worst of the education foundation. But my daughter is better off. She's in junior secondary, class two. But the fear that evolved me made me change my family plan. It has paralysed my mind for I know that in next six years to come my daughter would be on her way to higher education and I'm afraid I cannot*

*face the financial challenges considering my salary-level and also, to think that my wife had a car accident eight months ago and the doctor said that she may not be able to walk in time. I am now waiting for my daughter to reach eighteenth year of age for me to introduce her to **financial agency**. This wasn't how I planned it. I wonder where you were when I newly left school."*

After reading his mail, I could not talk. There was nobody to talk to. So I sat motionless, and stared at my thirteen inches laptop screen. I knew I started higher education in 2005, and I also knew that the mailer was disheartened when he wrote those words. Then I also wished he had met some other person, or had read from some other financial guiding books. **After Schooling**, only the strong-willed will continue. The second mailer wrote, "*Well, you have indeed impacted, thanks for your handout. As for me, it's late, it's no longer necessary, but I will make copies of it and share to my friends.*" I continued reading until I met a writer who wrote to me saying "*If you think you can write handout-notes to pass fear to people, well, good for you. But I will get employed gainfully and marry the woman of my choice, and we will have children whom we'll love such much, and then life goes on.*"

I did not bother; he was not the only one who feared life after school. Whether you think you can or you think you cannot, you're right. As a youth, life will present you with two rigid options. One is chances to meet opportunities and the other is chances to make your choices, to select the best one for your **desire**. No one will do that for you; only you will decide which one. The method by which you may alter your understanding about life to make these choices is as a result of listening to your inner audience. Job opportunity does not guarantee success in real life without the application of the basic ***principles of living success*** towards some worthy ***desire(s)***. Yet, everybody fears unemployment instead of failure. Through the medium of properly made study to discover the hidden possibilities within man, and justice which regulates his life, I discovered that youths have failed to recognize that they are actually three-in-one body, and all the affairs of man is generating efforts through the aid of the mind (inner man). This discovery of 'three-in-one body' has explained, in a common knowledge and understanding, to few men, that man owns himself. In a simple explanation, man is the person he thinks he is, he is the person he really is, and he is also the person he will become in time to come. But before a young man becomes that person he desires to become, there comes a time to think in every young man's life, a time to take that ultimate decisions and also make those choices:

"Now, there is no job opportunity what do I do?
"Now, I'm gainfully employed what do I do next?
"When do I leave my parents' house?"
"When do I begin to raise my own family?"
"Is this job what I will do for the rest of my life?" and so on.

This is where your choice(s) will affect and influence certain episodes of your life, till the rest of your life. "Life is the sum of your choices." Albert Camus. Through the application of perfectly made choices, man is **made**, and through the application of wrongly made choices, man is **unmade**. Between these two extremes are lots of graded characters, and man is the creator and the master of all his characters. Success is as a result of self-understanding and inner adjustment which enables man to exercise his self-control over any venture. It comes as a result of your ability to govern your mind.

Letter To Parents

Parents, I write to you, not because I want to blame you, but because you have also known it from the beginning. As a sharpened sword is in the hands of a great warrior, so are the youths in the hands of destructive fate where unemployment and financial illiteracy are the issues. Every river flows into the sea, but the sea is not yet full. Guide the youths like an egg till a lasting time. Their eyes can never see enough to be satisfied. Verily I tell you, most employees are working and labouring for lesser than they are worth. It is not sufficient to let down what you have suffered putting them (youths) through school. Youths become calm and better in the measure that they understand and believe in their own vision, and parents aiding them to attain them. For lack of such knowledge, few parents nowadays pay little or no regard to what their children say to them. The old-fashion of respect for the young is fast dying out. It is as good as waiting for tomorrow while today wastes away. Youths demand nothing but the future as its promise. I remembered that my father was building a duplex when I was seeking loan to aid my career after school; he never bothered. Nature hands over happiness to parents who understand that every man is a ruler who rules over his mind to see his children succeed. This observation was neither made by I, Ekeh Joe Obinna only, nor did I stress it alone. Hillary Rodham Clinton understood this issue when he says "No government can love a child, and no policy can substitute for a family's care. But at the same time, government can either support or undermine families as they cope with moral, social and economic stresses of caring for children."

Do not leave the youths vulnerable in the wilderness of unemployment because they cannot be young forever.

They are the results of your long and patiently emitted efforts in self-control over the years. They are already successful. In life, upon the commandment of nature, every man's success begins in the womb of his pregnant mother, death is failure. Stand for the youths, for what you understand and believe, even if it means standing alone. It is not just sufficient to tell them, "Go and find a safe job" as days go by. Government can do just but the ones they are doing, they cannot do all. If the government of a country is slacking, there is a big situation but if the parents of the youths go home feasting all night long, there is a big problem.

Parents, leaders, opposition to government is an attack to streets. How do you feel the youths feel about unemployment? Can you describe the life you lead? Do you, for instance, have certain principles or standards guiding all your actions? Or do you take life just as it comes, from one situation to the next or from day to day? We can support our youths because their problem is not just job opportunities, but to support them not to fail in any venture. Do it, it's all right with God. I have written to you, parents, because you lack equity in fraternity, and you're 16.2 percent responsible for the rising number of unemployment in the land, hence increasing crimes in society. A king may rule thousands, but cannot rule the minds of the youths. Their success is not in the hands of the leaders but in the foundation of their own thought. Lives that dwell in the ocean of truth and lots of possibilities are being delayed, daily, from manifesting their innate potentials.

What kind of life do you speak or dream for your children? Do you dare to realize it, or help them to realize it? We all know people who lose what is beautiful, many sour their lives, and some ruin their own possibilities. There are still those who destroy their balanced lives and make bad blood. The eyes of the youths cannot see enough to be satisfied. Great majority of them have grown too high in business ventures, and today, they are down below their own feet. They have not learnt from you, parents, whom humanity has taught a lot in self education.

What reasons have youths to accumulate knowledge and skills in educational institutions if the visions which they often visualize do not undergo a lasting transformation AFTER SCHOOLING? Youths are always the masters even when they have drained and exhausted their strength, they continue to manifest. But in their exhaustion, they are like great gladiators who surrendered their swords and other weapons and pleaded for their lives. Yet, they are as precious as curtains in a king's palace. Their senses of duty towards society remain stronger than their wish not to do whatever society likes. Parents, you are still not successful till you make nobody a somebody; that is why you're ahead. Success is the number of people who become successful through your aid.

Eight

JUSTICE AND POSSIBILITIES

There is so much trouble going on in the journey of life and living success. As you go through it you'll see that there's so much that we don't understand. "I think everybody should get rich and famous, and do everything they ever dreamed of so they can see that it's not the answer." - Jim Carrey. It will be better to live normal life. If you dig a pit, you'll fall into it. If you marry a nagging wife into your house, you will prefer to sleep on the roof. Man is the product of his choices. This life does not last forever. Judgement is brought on man on daily basis by nature. If you seek success, examine your idea because unexamined business idea is not worth venturing into. Therefore be careful when you begin to trade on the path. Everything will be all right if you ***keep moving***.

Life is good. It will be boring without trials and tribulations. I wouldn't have approached creative writing if I have no calling from God. Yet, I have experienced littleness and inferiority owing to, perhaps, the fact that life has a purpose. But the only thing that makes sense after all is being successful. And yet, there is no limit to things man can acquire.

If you have read to this page, then low self-esteem is not one of your problems. Put it in mind that no man will possess another man's wealth, and no man has ever seized another man's wealth. Every thought in man's mind, be it a bad or a good one, will not fail to produce its seeds on man and shape his circumstances. Let man consider his thoughts and affirmation. If you help no one, no one will help you. Man is better than animal because he has kinsman. A good reputation is better than expensive lifestyle, so be cautioned. A successful man will reap the good result of his earnest efforts for the number of people who become successful through his aid.

If living things do not exist, non-living things will last for eternity. Believe that nature has the ability to cause every man to gravitate to his success if man obeys the ***laws of prosperity***. In the light of this knowledge, understand that success is around the corner; therefore do not let your schooling interfere with your education. A time will come when the majority of school leavers will go into becoming business owners. Any one who is employed will be regarded as uneducated man. And this is how it should be if learning institutions have done their parts. If success is not achievable, failures won't bother. Obey the commandment and keep your desire under control. The wealthier you become, the more mouths you must feed. So agree that in less there is more. Too much wealth will wear you out. Death awaits both the richest and the poorest man. That is the only thing that doesn't make sense about life. We all have to suffer great pains and after all, we die. And it doesn't make sense dying a richest man when no one will offer to get in the bed with you when you die. Life is just like that. It is not an easy thing to succeed, yet it doesn't make any sense to succeed alone. And if success does not exist, failure will be a difficult thing to achieve.

The body obeys the operation(s) of the mind. The mind obeys the commandment(s) of the natural law. The natural law is in harmony with the Spiritual Law. The Spiritual Law provides the law of spiritual being- man. It does not promise freedom and rest at night, for man will (and he always does) go unconscious at night from the exhaustion of the day. No mind has ever stood idle. Had it been there is no night-time, man will still fall unconscious during the long day from weakness and exhaustion. Life is just like that. If pains were romance, then life is very, and always romantic. You are still nobody till you make nobody a somebody. If you accept bribes, your character is ruined and your future is complicated. Every man is your brother. Choose madness rather than unsuccessful life.

I was unmade, that was why I cured my mind and became successful. There is something else I have discovered that is more bitter than death women. They are moved by **_desire(s)_** unknown to men that trust in them. Their hearts are like prison yards where both the prison warder is also put behind closed gates. They may support you to succeed yet help you to fail, but real love is all about good friendship, be plain.

Secondly, I also discovered something more painful than child bearing men. They are the only hunters who hunt when not hungry. The richer you become, the more protection you must seek. Life is just like that. Because when everything goes to hell, and majority of people leave from your life, there are certain people who may not want to lead you, and they may not also want to follow you, they simply hold your hand and walk with you step by step. These are your friends and family members. But when you're on top, there is envy. Verily I tell you, every man is a man of success for success begins in the womb of every pregnant woman. Death is failure which no man can conquer; because life, with or without success, is a continuous progress to death. And God will judge the rich, yet judge the poor. But if you cannot help the poor do not hurt them. Correct me if I'm wrong, hasn't the thick straight line between poverty and prosperity gotten thicker? If you work too much, you will sleep too little. Yesterday is gone, put your desire under control. All man gained for being so rich is knowledge that he has wealth. You leave the world with nothing.

"It doesn't make sense dying a richest man when no one can offer to get in the bed with you when you die." - Ekeh Joe Obinna.

If you have reverence for the Lord you will be successful anyway. Spend but don't spend all for you can never tell how much setback you may experience tomorrow, yet no man is your real enemy.

A king may rule thousands but cannot rule the minds of the youths. Every man can freely rise to the height of his imagination. Start now, it's all right with God. At the end of life, when you stand before God on the Judgment Day, you will freely say to God, "Please wait, I used all the talents you gave me." You should leave the world with people who shall become successful through your aid.

Sometimes at midnight, I put on my lamp as to see success. I have hated no man and I have seen no man hate me. They simply do not understand most of the things I do. Understanding is all we need. Choose knowledge rather than the richest goldmine. Unemployment has never been a reality, and unsuccessful life is worse and more painful than child bearing. You can, if you wish. If you are an intelligent person you will understand that a failure is a successful man in time to come, so **Keep Moving**. When you work for something, something will work for you. Do not fail to segregate the workings of your brain from the workings of your mind. At the end you will beat your chest and say, "*I have tried*." Every man can embrace the joy and happiness of living success. Do not spend a night alone without a single thought, because if you do your assignment at night, before you will continue the next morning, there will be success.

There is judgement and commandment given to man. Help as much as you can and you won't lack help of any kind. Young people, life is one big party when you're still young. Let wretchedness find its false container elsewhere. There is no limit to things you can acquire, but too much wealth will make you vulnerable. Learn from the way ants live. They have no leader, no ruler, yet they store up their foods together during summer, getting ready for the winter. You can't be young forever. You are going to your final resting place. Do not say the Lord has not blessed you. Success is an affair of the mind, failure is that of head. I'm just here to remind you that every human's life is a bold and delicate projection of the eternal into the temporal. Life is not a rehearsal. As a youth, what remains now is half of an extra time. So, remember your creator in the days of your youth while you can. Every man suffers great loss and failure owing to lack of appreciation. If you desire to be loved, love and be loveable. Soon, the light of the sun, the moon, and the stars will grow dim for you. Then your arms, your legs will grow weaker. Your teeth will be too few to chew meat, and your eyes will not see everything any more. If you call a doctor, you will pay expensively and yet, nature will make walking difficult for you. Nature is an art of

God. You will not remember your wealth again, and by then, new things will emerge, and all ***desires*** would be gone. What you have acquired would be outdated and your troubles would spread faster than bacteria. If you are sick with dangerous virus, be happy. Soon, other more troublesome diseases will emerge. Life is good. Every one of us is going to his final resting place. ***Be strong***.

www.ingramcontent.com/pod-product-compliance
Lightning Source LLC
Chambersburg PA
CBHW071503040426
42444CB00008B/1465